About the Author

My name is Brian Keelan and I started smoking in 19.. the age of fifteen. Back then, cigarettes were 40 cents a pac

Today I am a survivor (so far) of a forty ye r smoking and I have been smoke-free since June 6th, 200(

I was finally able to quit smoking by using or ? of the techniques on the market today. Laser Therapy. A iorty fiv minute session and it was all over.

No problemo.

After I quit, I became fascinated by just what had happened to me. What was different about this attempt from all the other times that I tried to quit. Was it just the type of assistance I received? Was Laser therapy really that good?

Although I fully endorse Laser Therapy as an excellent way to help you stop, I don't think it was the therapy alone that did it.

This time, I had two major things going for me when I took the laser therapy:

1: I was absolutely determined to quit. No turning back.

2: I believed I would succeed this time. That's because I knew there was no other way. This time failure was not an option.

And this time I did succeed because when I walked out of the laser therapy session I did not *want* to smoke any more. Ever again.

This is my story of how I got there and how you can get there too. How you too can be free.

FREE AT LAST

Published by:

B.A.K. Publishing
A Division Of:
Keelans Audio/Video Centre Inc.

Printed In Canada

ISBN 0-9683764-1-X

Distributed by:

Hushion House Publishing Ltd.
36 Northline Rd.
Toronto, Ontario M4B 3E2

Orders:

Canada: Phone: 1-866-485-5556
           Fax: 1-866-485-6665

USA: Phone: 1-888-408-0301
      Fax: 1-717-568-8307

I dedicate this book to:

My Mother, Virginia Keelan

"Look Ma. Top o' the world."

and

My Son and Daughter-in-Law
Ned and Kim Keelan

"Please don't ever smoke again."

Contents

Foreword

Introduction

My Life as a Smoker

Quitting Time

The Stages

The Aftermath

Stopping vs. Quitting

Some people stop smoking. Others quit. There is a difference. A big difference.

When you *stop* smoking, you still *want* to smoke. You get the cravings and want to smoke a cigarette to relieve them. You think to yourself how nice it would be to smoke. You wish that you could smoke. Down deep you know it would not be a good thing for you but nonetheless it would still be great to have one. You aren't really convinced that it's over. You hope it's over but you still *want* a cigarette.

In the past, when I stopped, I never really, truly believed that my cigarette smoking was over. I hoped it was over. But way down deep, I did not believe that I would go the rest of my life without a cigarette. Why? Because, I still *wanted* a cigarette. Eventually I always gave in.

On June 6th, 2000, I quit smoking. This time I had no desire to smoke. I was then and am today, convinced that I will never, ever smoke another cigarette. Because I no longer *want* one. It is over. Never again.

The "smoking cessation" business is a one hundred million dollar a year industry in Canada. It is a billion dollar industry in the USA. One of the reasons this industry is doing so well is the relapse factor. In 2003, over 30 million North Americans did try to quit smoking, yet history shows that only 3% of the people who smoke will successfully *quit* forever.

I believe that most people who smoke wish they didn't. Many of them have tried to quit and failed. They *wanted* to quit. They were *afraid* of what would happen if they didn't quit. But like me, they didn't really *believe* they could do it. And until you *believe* you can do it, you won't.

You need help. And you need more than a pill, a patch, a herbal tonic, a session of hypnosis, acupuncture, laser therapy or anything else they come up with. You need to get yourself beyond just *wanting to quit*. You need to get to a point where you are not only *determined to* quit, but you *believe* that you *can* quit.

You need to get ready.

This book will help get you ready to quit. The techniques that I will tell you about worked for me, a forty year, pack-a-day smoker. Others have tried it and it worked for them as well. Some of them even quit cold turkey solely because of the deep convictions this story gave them that:

> **A:** They *had* to quit.
> **B:** They *could* do it.

After reading this book, your belief that you *can and must quit*, coupled with your *determination to quit* will be the factors that will get you over the hump. That belief and determination were by far the most powerful aspects of this approach for me. There are three basic reasons for this:

1: Logic. I did all of the math. There is no logical reason I can come up with that will support my decision to smoke. It is the dumbest way to spend a lot of money that there is.

2: Fear. I don't want my life to end until it's over and I'm not real good with the whole 'pain' thing. Lung cancer and heart disease scare the daylights out of me.

3: Anger. I am morally, intellectually and physically outraged with all of the people who make money off of this product.

Those factors of *logic*, *fear* and *anger* will combine to move you to the point where you will do whatever it takes to quit smoking forever.

When that happens, all you need to do
is choose your *'quit'* method and the date.
I know this will work for you because it worked for me.
Knowing that it worked for me will help you believe
that now you, like me, can finally be free.

FREE AT LAST!

The "10" factor:

I live in Sarnia, Ontario, Canada.

I am a Canadian but I have lived on the U.S. border all my life. I have spent a lot of time in the U.S. I grew up watching their television programs, rooting for their teams, seeing their movies, vacationing in their country and have lots of friends and relatives in the U.S.

The data I am using came from both sides of the border. Since the US market is roughly ten times the size of the Canadian market and the basic lifestyles of the two countries are quite similar; I have found over the years that the data of one country generally extrapolates to the other country using the number, (what else?) 10.

Therefore if you are an American, multiply the Canadian figures by 10 to get a close approximation of the US data. If you are a Canadian divide the US figures by 10 to get the Canadian numbers.

If you want to nitpick the data, you do not have a grip on the point here. There is a lot of money involved in smoking. The government and big business get the money.

You smoke. **You** lose your health. **You** die early. **You** die in pain. And **you** pay a lot of money for the privilege.

That is the point here. You may want to argue with some of my figures but you cannot argue with my conclusion: it is not only very unhealthy to smoke, it is stupid!

You must quit! Now!
Or you will die 15 years too early.

(That's in Canadian or American years.)

Introduction

Here are 5 emotions you will experience as you read my story.

1: Remorse.

You've wasted a lot of money. When you '**do** *all* **the math,**' you will realize just exactly how much money you have 'invested' in this habit. The logical part of your brain will kick in as it dawns on you just what you had to do to get this money and then you will start to think about what you could have done with that money if you had 'invested' it somewhere else.

You will then agree with this expression; "Smoking is one choice you will live to regret." If you're lucky you will only regret it for an instant as you realize that the heart attack you are having which is now killing you, could have been avoided if you hadn't smoked. There isn't one smoker out there who doesn't know that.

One of the great inventions of the 20th century has to be an increased lifespan. We are living longer than ever before. Current data suggests that the average North American male lives for 72.8 years and the female lives 78.5 years.

And it's getting longer every day. **If you don't smoke.**

Wouldn't you regret the fact that your life span had been increased by ten to fifteen years through modern technology and you then handed the fifteen years back to the tobacco industry. That's just got to induce a little remorse in a person.

2: Fear

You are going to die fifteen years earlier than a non-smoker. Every cigarette you smoke costs you five minutes of your life. About the time it takes to smoke the cigarette. If you are lucky you will have a heart attack and die on your way to the floor. Still fifteen years earlier than if you hadn't smoked but it will be a nice quick little death. If you're lucky.

If you're not that lucky then the last five to seven years of your life will be a living hell. And *then* you will die fifteen years too early. And you will have paid a lot of money for that privilege which will only add to your pain during those last years.

If that doesn't scare the daylights out of you, put the book down, go have a cigarette and get some psychiatric help. You need it. Tell the shrink you have some kind of masochistic death wish type of thing.

3: Anger:

You will be angry about a number of things.

A: You have been deceived and manipulated by the most devious and unscrupulous people on this planet. The tobacco industry, the advertising industry and your very own governments have conspired to take your money and now they will slaughter you.

B: What should really add some fuel to that fire is that, after they have killed you, they need to replace you because they want and need your money. They are addicted to profit.

C: That's when they go after your kids. Young people are pretty good at being cavalier about health matters. The people who market the cigarettes know that. They spend billions of dollars creating an illusion of 'cool' that your kids will 'buy' into. Go to www.Rense.com and look at their articles on smoking to see the lengths to which they will go to get our kids to smoke. And you thought Hannibal Lecter was evil. I'm sure he could take lessons from the people who market these products.

But, do not despair oh ye of little faith. As you read my story and learn abut the quitting process, these feelings of logic, fear and anger will merge to build a feeling of;

4: Hope:

As you begin to *see* and then *believe* that there is a way out. The "suits" at the tobacco companies and the "elected" political people who have played along with them are no longer going to have any power over you. You will be ready and able to quit this terrible habit/addiction.

As the momentum builds it will soon be followed by the

5: Joy:

The absolute joy of victory you will feel when you become an ex-smoker. You didn't just stop. You quit.

- You have beaten the toughest *addiction* of them all. Nicotine.

- You have beaten the meanest, most devious bunch of schemers on this planet. The tobacco industry. You can take pride in being one of the elite 3% who have beaten this addiction.

And the very best part is that actually, it was easy.
Real easy.
You ain't ever gonna smoke again.
Because now, you are free baby!

FREE AT LAST!

And then!

As an added bonus, you will have a **wonderfully profound feeling of accomplishment.** The kind that only comes with the knowledge that you can now do something that you never before *believed* you could do.

- What other things can you do now?
- You will have more money in your pocket.
- You will be healthier. A lot healthier.
- Everything will taste better.
- You will smell better. A lot better.
  (Ask a friend who doesn't smoke.)

Your sex life will improve. You'll not only enjoy it more. You'll want it more and because you don't smell like an old ashtray you'll probably get more.

You will enjoy life more and feel better knowing that you have beaten the odds. They were stacked against you and you beat them. Now you can take that extra money and do something you want to do.

You no longer have to feed the coffers of the lowlifes in the tobacco industry and the various government knobs who know that you will pay any price to smoke.

When you quit, you will feel like you've beaten the house. And you have. I know that feeling. Because I did it. Every day I think about the fact that I have quit smoking forever and if I can do that, I can do a whole bunch of other stuff that I never thought I could do. And do you want to know the best part?

It was easy.

This book will not tell you what support method to use in order to help you quit. There are lots of proven and effective ways to do that. But every one of them will say that in order for their product or technique to work you have to be 'ready.' And that's the stumper.

How do you get ready?

By ready, I don't mean, "I *want* to quit."

I mean "Dammit, I'm *going* to quit! And I'm going to quit now. I do not want to smoke anymore."

Your problem right now today, is not that you can't quit. Your problem *is* that you don't *believe* that you can quit. Once you *believe* that you can quit, then brother, there is no reason to continue smoking. You are there.

You will quit.

I tried to quit lots of times and failed and I know why I failed. I failed because I didn't *believe* way down deep inside that I could do it, and like the man says, and the tobacco marketers are well aware of, **"If you think you can or you can't, you're probably right."**

When I finally did quit, I was ready. **I believed.** This book will tell how I got ready. At the end of this book, you will be ready too. Your head will be in that space where you can say with full confidence that: **"I am going to quit smoking. Now!"**

Instead of being a person who will do whatever it takes to get a 'fix,' you will now do whatever it takes to stop.

When you are that fired up about something, you can accomplish great things. You will look back on your victory over this addiction as one of the great moments in your life.

That great moment when you knew for sure that you were Free.

FREE AT LAST!

So.
Read 'on Macduff.
And damned be him who first cries,
'Hold, enough!'

A Few Thoughts

Forty years and a hundred thousand dollars later, I did it! I broke the shackles that had bound me since I was fifteen years old. I quit smoking! A pack-a-day habit that had enslaved me for forty years has now been completely and utterly vanquished.

I am saved! Delivered at last from the depths of depravity, moral degradation and, as the math will point out, the dumbest financial decision I ever made.

As you read this story you will see that my addiction to nicotine and your addiction to nicotine are very similar. How I got started and the way the habit took over my life, is a tale that is not unique to me.

Cigarettes ruled my life for 40 years in the same way they now rule yours. For 40 years I never did anything or went anywhere, without making completely sure that I would be able to smoke a cigarette whenever and wherever the urge to do so came upon me.

If you could simply butt out and walk away from it, I'm sure you would. I would have. But you can't. Because you're addicted.

To you right now, the idea of going the next day, let alone the rest of your life, without a cigarette is unthinkable. **No matter how high they raise the price, 97% of you who smoke today, are going to keep paying and smoking until finally this filthy habit releases you or - you release yourself from it.** Believe me, the people who sell you the cigarettes will not help you quit. They want your money!

Their PR departments may create the illusion that they will help you quit, yet in their labs they are actually researching ways of making this terrible habit more physically addictive. It's a *'the higher the price the deeper the addiction needs to be,'* phenomenon. The governments realize that they can tax the daylights out of cigarettes, and the addicts (smokers) will still keep smoking. Since the tobacco industry can write off the research thanks to their 'inside' position with the government, they will spend whatever is necessary to find new techniques of deepening your addiction. "What the heck man, it's all a write-off."

If you're really lucky, you'll have a heart attack and be dead before you hit the floor. If you aren't that lucky, then surely you must know that you are in for a painful, agonizing and totally senseless death.

All of that, courtesy of the tobacco industry, which incidentally you are also making rich beyond their wildest dreams.

Some people have quit **'cold turkey'** and it always made me crazy to hear about it.

Why couldn't I do that? What strength did they have that I didn't?

Today, as I put my habit farther and farther behind me, I've come to understand the process that finally got me over the hump and off that deadly weed. Forever.

You've got to get your head into a certain space or frame of mind if you will. When you do that, it can and will happen. Once you're there, you may not be able to just butt out and walk away. You may decide to use an outside method to help you, just as I did.

And that's okay. Whatever it takes.

But, until you get your head into the right place, you can take all the pills and patches and miracle cures you want, I believe the odds are against you being able to stop smoking with the firm conviction in your mind that you will never, ever smoke another cigarette again.

And when I say that, I mean joyfully, go the rest of your life without a cigarette, knowing that now, you are finally:

FREE AT LAST!

That's where I am today. And will be for the rest of my life. I now bitterly regret the years that I did smoke because I realize that I could have gotten here a lot sooner.

I just needed to know what I know now. What's in this book. Believe me, if you want to quit, **this book will show how to get there.**

If I had done it earlier, I'd have a lot more money in the bank today. I'd look younger. I'd be in better physical condition. My whole life would be different.

The really sad part is that if some of my friends had quit, they'd be alive today. **You can bet that not one of them died without *totally* regretting the fact that they smoked.**

Ask John Wayne. Humphrey Bogart, Walt Disney, Yul Brynner and the Marlboro Man. Oh wait now. You can't. Thanks to cigarettes, they're all dead. Just like you'll be if you don't stop.

If you got a chance to ask them; "What's the dumbest thing you ever did in your whole life?" What do you think they would tell you? Do you think they might say, "The dumbest thing I ever did in my life was to start smoking."

With these thoughts in mind let me begin to explain the process that set me on the journey to a life without cigarettes.

Then you can do it too.

CHAPTER 1
Why I Started

I started smoking back in the fifties. I was fifteen years old. Back then, *Life* magazine and their ilk used to run big, splashy ads showing guys like John Wayne smoking a *Camel*. Dressed in his cowboy duds, the Duke was standing tall and lookin' good. Tellin' us all to *'listen and listen tight'* as he told us how much he loved smoking those Camels and how we should too if, *'ya knew what wuz good fer ya.'*

Casablanca. Great movie, and probably the best smoking commercial in history. It did more to promote smoking as a cool thing to do than any other movie I've ever seen. And it's been faithfully watched by millions for over fifty years. Sam playing piano in the background. Bogie sitting there with his drink and that ever present cigarette dangling from his lips.

I was a sixteen-year old Catholic schoolboy, and thus never encouraged to actually think for myself, so naturally I figured, "Wow! The Duke. And Bogie. They're pretty cool guys. I could be cool like that too if I smoked."

Besides, most of the priests smoked. Throw in James Dean and I was a marked man.

Twenty-five years later I saw the Duke on the Academy Awards as he was getting ready to die from lung cancer. It was shocking. He looked awful. I've always wondered how the people at Camel must have felt when they saw him that night. They probably rationalized their guilt with thoughts of stock options.

I can also remember an ad featuring *'macho?'* movie star, Rock Hudson. Sitting in a very manly chair, in a very manly log cabin, with his very manly hunting dog, wearing a very manly bright red flannel shirt and urging us in a very manly way to smoke *Camels* for "more pure pleasure."

The point here is that the tobacco companies will hire people you like, who do cool things on screen but whose real life is absolutely nothing like the life you see them lead on screen. (Believe me. I was shocked to find that Rock Hudson's real life was nothing like that macho image he portrayed on the screen.)

These people are called 'Role Models.' The tobacco companies will pay these people to smoke their brand of cigarettes and portray these people as the epitome of the type of person you want to be or should want to be, unless you are some kind of a pathetic loser.

This, they figure, will help you rationalize your decision to smoke. Maybe not if you are a full blown adult. But if you are fourteen, fifteen, sixteen or even younger, then it's a whole different ballgame.

Especially if you have parents who do smoke. Not only like my parents did, but also as my wife and I did right in front of our own children.

I was 'recruited' by the use of role models who broke down my psychological resistance to the act of smoking. Meanwhile people like my teachers, my parents and their friends, who by the way, smoked, would tell me *not* to do it because it was bad for me.

Mixed messages here wouldn't you say? The ads said (and still say to this day) that cool people do it and you will be cool too, if you do it. You can be just like them. All you have to do is smoke.

And if you want to be really cool, smoke this brand. The Duke does. Bogey does. DeNiro does. Jack does. Brad does.

Come on man. Don't be a total frigging loser, just have one of these. You'll be cool. You'll see.

That's when the tobacco companies have you right where they want you.

Today they use free-base nicotine in cigarettes with extra strong hits of it during the first few drags. Have you ever heard of freebase crack cocaine? With one hit of crack cocaine you're addicted. It gives you a bigger hit (which of course is why they do it) and thus deepens the existing addiction or hooks the rookies. Same idea when they free-base tobacco. They are using a technique that they learned from hard-core drug users. Ask Richard Pryor.

What's really awful is that today, they are using this technique on our kids. Now I don't know about you, but personally I think that sucks. Bigtime. That I cannot abide.

Now that I know *how* and *why* I got started, if there is one thing I would like to do in this life that really matters, it would be to motivate and help people to kick their habit and help to stop young people from ever getting on it.

Role models and mixed messages.

The cool people said it was good for me. **My parents said it was bad for me but they did it too, so could it really be that bad?** Besides, I figured they just didn't want to see me having all that fun. They figured I couldn't handle it. After all, we were Catholic and if it didn't hurt it wasn't fun and therefore it was not good for you. And you have to admit, smoking feels good when you start.

I never had any mixed messages about heroin or opium for instance. No cool role models there. Right from the start it was shown to me to be a stupid and very dangerous thing to do and I can't remember ever seeing or hearing anything that alluded otherwise. I was never, ever tempted to fool around with that kind of stuff.

But the cigarette companies had the governments in their back pockets. There was and is, a lot more money involved in the tobacco game than there was in the heroin game. So the cigarette companies basically had it all their way. "Just let the governments in on the deal and they'll let us do anything we want."

They sold the concept by simply urging me to, "Just try one. See how good it is. How nice it makes you feel." That's their game plan. They urged me to do it over and over. Thousands and thousands of times. They even got Fred Flinstone and Barney Rubble to do a Winston commercial. The tobacco company knobs will probably claim that they were going after my parents with that ad but I think that's like trying to tell me that a fart is a breath of fresh air.

"Winston tastes good. Like a cigarette should."

"Hey Fred, it not only tastes good but it does feel kind of good too doesn't it?"

"Right you are Barn."

Once I "tried it" a few times, the addiction/habit process took over. Just as they knew it would. Now it was only a matter of which brand I smoked or rather, which role model I identified with. The one with the coolest advertising won the customer.

Once I tried it, the next question was: **Am I a *Marlboro* Man or would I walk a mile for a *Camel*?**

A Role Model Story

When I was a lad of twelve, my Dad took me on a fishing trip to the French River in the Georgian Bay area of Ontario. It was early in the summer, just after school ended. Nobody at the lodge we stayed at had boated a muskie yet and the local tradition had it that the guy who caught the first "legal" muskie of the season would win a bottle of scotch.

He would then sit on the dock well into the night with the other less fortunate guests. He would drink the scotch and share it with them as they dutifully listened to the catcher of the muskie, recount his bravery in slaying the small savage fish which got larger and more savage as the scotch was depleted.

On our last night there, my dad caught a muskie. A big one. No scotch was needed to describe the size of the fish. As we lay the fish on the dock for weighing and measurement, an older man stood by looking on with a sad, wistful smile on his face. He asked my dad where he caught the fish.

My dad told him all about the little bay with the great rock just below the surface about twenty feet off the shore. How just as the sun was setting we had trolled by and, "Wham!" This fish hit the lure and the battle was on.

The old man listened intently as my dad described his battle and even gave me credit for helping him boat the fish. He told him how I had taken the net, scooped the fish from behind and swooped it into the boat in one motion.

The older man smiled wistfully and said, "You know, I'm sure I caught that same fish last year in that exact same spot where you caught him."

"Really," my dad said. "What happened?"

"Well, just like you did, I fought him for a good half hour and when I got him up to the boat he was tuckered out. That's when my stupid, shit-for-brains brother-in-law took the net and tried to scoop him into the boat. But unlike your son here, my brother-in-law tried the scoop from ahead of the fish. Well that fish just spit that lure into the net, flapped his tail and boom. He was gone."

"Oh no," my dad and I said at the same time.

"That's awful," my dad went on. "What did you do?"

"On not much. I just sat back down in the boat and lit a cigarette."

"Well that doesn't sound too bad. You handled it pretty well I'd say."

"Not really," the man replied as he took a drag. "I hadn't had a cigarette in twenty five years and I've been smoking a pack and half a day ever since."

It's a funny story. If you don't smoke.

It's a tragic one if you do.

CHAPTER 2

The Quitting Game

Over the years, I tried to quit many times. I actually became quite good at it. It eventually became a bi-monthly event for me, so I certainly had enough practice.

People would ask me, "What's the matter? Are you such a weak-minded individual that you can't quit this disgusting habit, which I am sure you must know will eventually kill you?"

Looking down my nose and sneering at them, I'd reply, "Don't be stupid. I can quit anytime I want. Hell, I already quit twice this month. And just to show you how strong-minded I really am, I'm going to quit right now."

I actually did stop once. For four very long months. As it turned out though, I didn't really quit. I just stopped for a while. After faithfully attending a three month Smoke Enders withdrawal program, I did stop.

For six weeks I carried a mason jar around with all the ashes and the butts of every cigarette I smoked during that period of time. It was disgusting. Each week I waited a little longer after I got up to smoke and stopped smoking a little earlier before bedtime. After 6 weeks, I stopped altogether.

But it wasn't enough. It wasn't really over. I had beaten the addiction but not the habit and even worse, I still had the *desire* to smoke.

Way down deep in the cockles of my heart, even down in the sub-cockle area, I never really honestly felt that I was going to go without a cigarette for the rest of my life. I *hoped* I would, but deep down I felt that I wouldn't. Sure I had a nagging fear in my gut that I would get lung cancer or something but that alone was not enough to give me the conviction I needed to say; "That's it. I quit. Never again."

That's because even though I had stopped smoking, **I still
wanted to smoke.** I didn't *need* one, but I *wanted* one. They
made me feel good. They relaxed me. I *knew* that it would be
bad for me so all I needed was a **'reason'** that would be strong
enough to overcome that feeling I had that doing so would be
bad for me.

Looking back on that period today, **I recognize the
rationalization process that I used** and if I can offer you any
advice at this time, it's that you should recognize that
rationalization is a big part of the process of 'keeping the habit,'
a.k.a. 'not quitting.'

The habit and the addiction will fight very hard in your
subconscious to maintain their position. That I believe is
because **your own personal ego does not want to admit that you
are weak.** It looks for rational reasons for you to fail and thus
postpone the inevitable moment that every smoker knows deep
down they will ultimately face;

"I wish to hell I'd never started because now I'm in big trouble because of it."

Four months later, **I finally did find the perfect excuse to
start back up again.** It was a psycho-social excuse. I usually
smoked when I was agitated or excited. It was a long-term
tendency to smoke when I 'felt' a certain way.

It was a true 'let's have a smoke' moment.

I went to the Royal Oak Theater in Detroit to see Thomas
'Hitman' Hearns fight 'Marvelous' Marvin Hagler. If you're
looking for a justifiable, rational excuse to fall off the no-
smoking wagon, just go to a smoke and testosterone-filled
arena with a bunch of hard-drinking, bloodthirsty guys to
watch a classic boxing match. It's not man at his best and it's
not man at his worst. It's more like man at his manliest.

(Or so he likes to think.)

Manly men doing manly things. Together. We'd all had a
big steak dinner and a few beers. We did not want to see 'The

Sound Of Music.' This was not a 'Fried Green Tomatoes' type of evening.

At the end of round one, arguably, one of the greatest rounds of boxing in the history of the 'sweet science,' the crowd was on fire. The guy beside me lit up a cigarette. I looked longingly at him as he took his first long drag.

Man it smelled so good. The moment was upon me. God that thing looked so good.

He offered me one.

I knew then it was over as I grabbed it. Eagerly.

"Thanks man." And started right back up. Just as if I'd never quit. **But, I did have a great 'excuse' though. Didn't I?** I mean it was such an exciting event that surely a cigarette was justified. Everybody else seemed to be doing it.

I mean, you had to be there. I'm sure you would have agreed that I did the right thing.

Didn't I?

It was more of a lifestyle thing than a habit or addiction thing. The addiction was long gone.

But what about the habit?

There was really no habit here to deal with. I had been to several fights before but not in the last few years. Ali-Fraser, Ali-Foreman that kind of thing. But, good fights are few and far between, so there was no real basis for a habit, and it was a part of my lifestyle. Get together with a bunch of guys and go do something like that.

It was not my first time in a situation like that. It was sort of like lighting up in the waiting room after the nurse tells you that your wife just had your son. You don't really cave in to a habit. **You cave in to the moment.** I know the drill. That's what I did that night.

The tobacco marketing people call it, *'positioning.'* You've seen it in commercials; "Get the long distance feeling." They show you a tender moment on TV that invokes a flood of memories that induce feelings. Other people will recall different memories but those memories will invoke similar feelings.

The theory is that you have your own feelings based on pleasant experiences and they are stronger motivators and unique to you. All they try to do in the commercial is present a situation that evokes those feelings. It was 'Miller Time!'

I was positioned perfectly to feel comfortable lighting one up. So I did. In doing so, **I began the short journey back to my physical addiction.** And when I did that, I re-inserted all my former habits and not being one to rest on the laurels of my personal status quo, I even developed some new habitual smoking situations to deepen my dependency on tobacco.

Who can I blame for this? The tobacco industry? Social pressure? The Media? The government? The Duke? Bogie? Anybody but me. Right?

It wasn't my fault.....Right?

I was a victim .... Right?

Poor little addicted, stupid me. *"Here pal, have a smoke. It'll calm you down."*

CHAPTER 3

Rationalization & Procrastination

The tools of the devil...and the tobacco companies.

At the age of forty-five, after attending the funeral of a forty four year old friend of mine who smoked and drank and then had one of those dead-before-he-hit-the-ground type of heart attacks, I once again rationalized my bad habits by promising myself I'd quit them all when I turned fifty. That's when I'd start to lose some weight, eat sensibly, quit smoking, exercise regularly and cut back on the booze.

It's funny. When you're young, you always think of the future as a long way off. The little voice would say, *"Hey, don't worry about that stuff now. If smoking kills you, it won't be for a long time. Forget about it. You can deal with that later. Relax. Have a cigarette."*

I went to the funerals of my boyhood heroes, contemporaries and even younger friends who died of emphysema, heart disease and lung cancer. I cried with their family and friends about how tragic it all was. How it did not have to happen. "If only they had been smarter and a little more disciplined, they would be here today." Then I went outside for a smoke.

I vowed that an early death would never happen to me. As I stood there, I rationalized that I was just smoking now to get me over this little 'stress-bump' in my life and then I would find a way to quit.

But how? Cold Turkey?

As a nice 'family' man from New Jersey once said to me, "Fuhgedaboudit."

Cold turkey was not an option. Much too painful. Too much personal discomfort for a person like me exercising my divine right to feel good whenever I wanted to. I was afraid of becoming too stressed with the cravings plus all the other stresses of my life.

Plus I'd gain weight!

That's it! Keep smoking and I'll have a nice way to deal with stress and I won't gain any weight.

Good thinking.

Cold Turkey could never work for me. Too much pain. **I needed a painless, stress-free way to do it.**

I tried the "patch," the "gum," subliminal audio-tapes, acupuncture and the "pill."

I was extensively hypnotized. Several times. Could not make it through one lousy day without a cigarette. I procrastinated. I rationalized. And... I continued to smoke.

The grim truth scared the daylights out of me but fear alone did not provide me with the strength or the will to stop.

- Fear of death before my time
- Fear of having people think I was stupid and weak
- Fear of pain
- Fear of leaving this life before I got done what I wanted to get done
- Fear of living a greatly reduced lifestyle

Not enough.

I could and did live with all that fear.

It's weird but smoking actually even helped me deal with the stress of that fear.

Then one day, before I knew it, I was looking at the short end of my fifty-fifth year. I wasn't young anymore. I was not only on the downward side of the hill, I was more than halfway to the bottom.

The future was this afternoon.

And I was still smoking.

Shit!

I always came up with a great excuse not to deal with the problem today.

I was a master at it.

Deep down inside, the sane part of me knew what I had to do. I knew that if I didn't quit, smoking would kill me. It was no longer a matter of 'if' it would happen, it had now become a matter of 'when' it would happen.

I knew that I had to learn to live without tobacco or I was going to die because of it. After spending a couple of years in a lot of physical pain and mental discomfort. Regretting the fact that none of this bullshit had to happen. I could have prevented it.

Me. The idiot now going through all this pain which is going to lead to my agonizing death made even more painful by the knowledge that I *could* have prevented it.

But, I had a lot of good, valid well-rationalized reasons for not doing it.

Didn't I?

Words To Live By?

A non-smoking, health fanatic, friend told me,

*"The one thing you should realize about smoking is that if it has any **positive** effect on you whatsoever, that effect will be that nothing at all will happen to you.*

However;

if something does happen to you as a result of your smoking habit, you can bet your ass you're not going to like it."

Another friend
really freaked me out;

"Have you ever seen anybody dying from lung cancer? It's a hell of a thing to see.

If you continue to smoke, you should pray that you'll die in a traffic accident.

It won't hurt nearly as much."

I've had more than a few nightmares thanks to those pretty little thoughts.

But, truth be told, I enjoyed smoking. It did make me feel good. It did help me relax. I found it easy to rationalize my addiction/habit by letting myself believe that I was just one of those types of people who were born to smoke.

My friends and relatives didn't let me get away with that and started coming down hard on me. "Dammit Keelan, if I wind up going to your funeral because you died of lung cancer, I will tell everybody that even though I loved you, will miss you terribly and had a lot of fun with you, you ****ing well deserved to die because you smoked! You stupid ass****! Now cut that **** out! Now!"

Out of respect for them I simply stopped smoking in front of them and told them that I took their advice and quit. But they could smell the stuff on me and continued coming down on me for it, so I quit hanging around them altogether. I figured I'd show those guys that they couldn't push me around.

I saved a lot of face there didn't I?

CHAPTER 4

How Bad Could It Get?

In the recent years of health conscious political correctness, I was relegated to standing outside in the cold, and lighting up along with my fellow addicts. Huddled together in the rain and the snow, we would joke about our banishment. But we stared at the ground when we did.

Either that or we looked away off into the distance. And asked inane, meaningless questions. "How about this weather, eh?" Anything to avoid acknowledging how we really felt.

Like outcasts. Losers.

But a little better after that last drag thank you very much.

We often wondered aloud why were we made to feel this way? I mean after all, we were paying our governments and some very large corporations a lot of money for the privilege of choosing to adopt this particular addiction.

We were supporting the economy.

Yet here we were being publicly humiliated, isolated and even ostracized for freely exercising, if not a god-given right, then at the very least a constitutionally-guaranteed right to provide ourselves with as long, as slow, as expensive, as early and as agonizing a death as we wanted?

We knew exactly how insane it was to be doing what we were doing and yet we still could not or even worse, would not quit. We all had a bona fide reason for smoking. We were hooked!

Twice, I went down the Middle Fork of the Salmon River in Idaho. A hundred and five mile, six day trip. Since it was wilderness territory, they would not let me leave any evidence that I had ever been there, except a footprint. No cigarette butts and for sure no ashes.

In order to feed my habit/addiction I carried some zip-lock bags with sand in them and flicked every ash of every cigarette into the bag. Then I put the butt into the bag with the ashes and put the bag in my duffel. I was embarrassed when all the non-smokers looked at me. Not with disgust but with pity.

I imagined them saying, "You poor pathetic dork. You're killing yourself. You know it and yet you subject yourself to this humiliation and make the tobacco companies rich. You are a real schmuck!"

The tobacco companies had us right where they wanted us. Standing outside, freezing our asses off and giving ridiculous amounts of our money to them in order to feel a little better for a little while.

I know I felt better. Didn't I? Don't you?

With these facts gnawing at our insides, eye contact amongst us was a little uncomfortable. You'd look at the other poor bastards out there smoking and see yourself.

Not a pretty sight.

No smoking at hockey games, baseball games, movie theaters, football games, restaurants, even rock concerts. You can do ecstasy, LSD, and 'shrooms at your seat. You can drink in the hallways, you can even do a little cocaine in the washrooms if you want. But hey! No smoking. It's bad for your health. You have to go outside to smoke.

They do that so you won't offend the politically correct alcoholics and drug addicts inside. They have rights too.

I remember standing outside the Silver Dome in Pontiac, Michigan. Inside, eighty thousand people were watching the Detroit Lions play the Dallas Cowboys. There must have been fifteen thousand people standing outside in the cold December drizzle at halftime. Smoking. All of us looking at each other in disgust and saying the same thing that they've all been saying since 1957;

"Goddamned Lions!"

Old smokers that never die.

It always used to give me a lift to see old people smoking. One time I saw this cute little old gray-haired lady sitting at a bar in the Flamingo in Las Vegas. She was nursing a coffee, playing video poker and smoking furiously. I approached her and said, "Gee, it's really great to see older people who smoke. It helps us younger smokers believe that we can smoke well into our twilight years and yet still survive the experience. You've obviously been smoking for a long time. Would you mind terribly if I asked you how old you are?"

With her cute wrinkled face scrunched into a smile, she replied, "I'm thirty seven."

The point here is that **cigarette smoking ages you more quickly than Father Time.**

On the plus side, you don't want to look too young when you die, so I suppose that the early aging thing doesn't make you look like a total loser when you're in the casket fifteen years before you should be. People will think you were older than you really were.

"Live fast, die young and leave a good-looking corpse."

James Dean smoked. Didn't really matter though. Those people never live long enough to worry about death from smoking. The reason is quite simple actually. They're idiots.

But they looked good. Problem is that they continue to this day to reinforce the smoking habit in younger people who actually believe that crap for a short while and when they finally do smarten up, it's too late.

They're hooked. Or worse yet. Dead.

The evil marketing plans of the tobacco industry have worked. And worked well.

Once upon a time:

I was sitting in the waiting room of the ultrasound department at a hospital with my daughter in-law. One of the people in waiting there was a guy I knew from high school. As we brought each other up to date on our lives, it came up in the conversation that his father had died at age seventy one. The father had smoked for thirty years and then quit at age fifty six. But, his grandfather had smoked from childhood until his death at age ninety four. He thought that was strange.

I told him that come to think about it, I remembered seeing a lot of old smokers back in my youth but that now, it was a rarity. He told me that it was because in those days they smoked tobacco that was almost organic in nature. In other words, no pesticides had been used to stop the bugs from eating away at the plants. Since tobacco was a product that was grown but not eaten like say carrots or corn, they can to this day use the heavy duty pesticides that have cyanide in them. The result was that the grower had a lot higher yield per acre

(I think you could spell that p-r-o-f-i-t).

However the deadly, toxic, cyanide-laden pesticide, over several generations of use, has now worked its way into the ecological system and is part of the soil nutrient in the tobacco plant itself. It's not just getting sprayed *on* the plant. It's actually growing *in* the plant. They call it 'systemic.' It becomes part of the plant itself.

Now, the tobacco companies can say that they don't add cyanide to the tobacco and in truth they may not. It's not like they pick it and add it in at the factory. They don't have to. It's already in the stuff! It's there when they get it from the growers.

It is little stories like this that the tobacco company PR people will say are false, but when you get down to street level, where the farmers and other people who actually do the work are, then you tend to hear the same kind of story from completely unrelated sources. I will never believe the tobacco

PR people since the very nature of PR departments is to take the truth and spread bullshit all over it that makes it look like the best stuff since sliced bread.

Another friend of mine, a customer who I did some work for, had congratulated me for stopping smoking. He went on to tell me that both his parents had died from cancer at young ages. His dad at 60, and his mother at 61. Neither of them smoked.

But they grew the stuff. He himself had never smoked even though he worked on his dad's farm as a kid. "Wouldn't ever smoke. I've seen the stuff they spray on tobacco. That's what killed my parents. They got cancer from mixing the stuff we sprayed on the tobacco plants."

I asked him, "Why did they spray that kind of stuff on tobacco plants?"

"Two reasons. To stop bugs from eating the plant and to make the plant grow faster and bigger. That way we could get more pounds of product for our dollar invested. The scary part is that a lot of the stuff we used was 'systemic.' That means it became a part of the plant for future generations."

That one scared the daylights out of me. The tobacco industry will never come straight out and tell us that they are doing these kinds of things. They will only deal with these issues 'after' we have discovered it and only after we have broken through all the barriers they constantly put in our way. They only do this for one reason.

Money.

I smoked 9,125 cigarettes a year!
That's an average of 760 per month!

It's much more shocking when you say it that way instead of saying, "I smoke a pack a day." I smoked in the car, at my desk, at my computer, reading the paper, on the can, on the phone, watching TV, with every coffee, with every drink, after dinner, before dinner and sometimes even, during.

Did you ever lie in bed at three in the morning and smoke a cigarette? I did. Every night.

Did you ever wake up in the morning and light one up before you even got out of bed? I did. Every morning.

What did you tell your kids when they asked you why you smoked?

"Well sweetheart. Daddy knows that smoking is a very bad thing to do and will probably give him lung cancer or heart disease or worse yet, both. Daddy knows that he is setting a bad example for you but you see, (give them the old sad face here) Daddy's addicted and he's too stupid and selfish to quit. But don't any of you kids start. It's a very baaaaad habit."

How did you feel when one of your own kids started smoking?

Stupid? I know that feeling.

I was forced to invoke parental rule #1:

"Do as I say, not as I do."

By doing this I was therefore able to transfer my internal anger at myself over to my kids, thus enabling myself to feel even stupider.

How would you feel if your own kid actually took your parental rule #1 advice and quit smoking? Cold-turkey. Would you keep right on smoking?

I did. Actually she quit because she was afraid it would damage her singing voice, not because of my hypocritical parenting techniques.

Big lesson there if you're paying attention. She just wanted something more than she wanted to smoke. If you want something bad enough that seems to make it easier to get through the rough spots.

As a result of her quitting, I was forced to re-transfer my anger toward my children for smoking back to myself since I no longer had any kids who smoked. Is that the act of a schmuck or what?

It's ironic. In fact it's more than ironic. It's moronic. As a teenager I hid my smoking habit from my parents and as a parent I was now trying to conceal my habit from my teenaged children. I didn't really fool anybody ...... Or did I?

I began to hate myself for my weakness. For ultimately acknowledging to myself and the world that I was powerless and unable to control my addiction. I lived with my fear of disease and my own self-loathing on that famous African river.

De Nile. Why?

Because I was afraid. **Afraid to commit myself to living the rest of my life without a cigarette.** That's really why I didn't quit. Sure the addiction was there but **the fear of living without it was greater than the fear of dying from it.** So I continued to procrastinate and rationalize.

And I smoked.

Quitting Time

CHAPTER 5

Salvation!

Then one evening while watching the Channel 7 News from Detroit, they ran a story about a little place in Windsor, Ontario that was attracting Detroiters in droves.

Why?

Because they were having a very high success rate when it came to helping people stop smoking. Their technique was called '**Laser Therapy.**' The TV guy exit-polled a couple of customers. The smiling people said that they had been very long-time heavy smokers and that this amazing little place had really helped them stop. One visit and it was over.

I thought to myself: '*Let me see now. Here we have long-time smokers, who are now completely free of the habit. Could this be my answer? The easy way out. No pain. Big gain. No withdrawal symptoms. No going crazy for a smoke. No more feeling like an outcast and a loser because I was too weak to 'Just Say No." All I do is give these nice Laser people some money and this evil addiction will go away? This is perfect man. Sounds too good to be true.*'

In my life, I have found that **anything that seemed too good to be true, was.** Just about every politician I have ever met or voted for as well as my first wife, most fast food, Bre-X, Enron, World Com, Arthur Andersen, IMClone, Tyco, O.J, Martha, all those ab machines and hair restoring elixirs and don't let me get started on the whole gasoline price thing. And as it turns out, French fries too.

Get my drift? I was too smart to get sucked in again by another easy way out thing. Wasn't I?

Within minutes, I was on the phone (1 800 807 8714)

I was most impressed when an actual live human being answered the phone. I told her, "Yes ma'am, my name is

45

Schmuck. Mr. All-Canadian Schmuck. How much for an appointment. I want one. Now!"

The young lady allowed as to how they were quite busy and it would be two months before they could get me in. **The cost would be three hundred and twenty five after-tax, you can not write them off, Canadian dollars.** The TV news spot had done its' publicity job and produced an incredible surge in demand.

I was not alone.

For the next two months I waited...... and smoked. I felt a little better though since I felt I had taken the first big step on the road to my own personal salvation.

The end was in sight.

A little advice:

One big thing I did and I recommend that you do it as well, is that once you have booked your quit date, **change the brand of cigarettes you smoke.**

1: I figured it would be easier to quit smoking a brand of cigarettes that I hated instead of a brand I liked or at least was used to. I switched to one of those low-tar, cave-your-skull-in-trying-to-get-a-decent-hit type cigarettes. They were awful and I hated them.

2: This also reinforced my feeling of personal accomplishment since I felt I had taken one more progressive step towards my ultimate goal. Stopping smoking forever.

Start doing some homework!

I spent some time on the Internet trying to do some research on the process. Didn't find much on laser therapy but I found a whole bunch of other stuff.

Go to the search section of a search engine like say, 'Google.' Once you have their search engine on your screen, type in 'cigarette smoking.' You will have several pages of web sites to choose from. I found 823 web sites that proclaimed in detail the dangers of smoking, the hypocrisy of the industry and the government and even one that related cigarette smoking to cancer of the penis!

That's right guys, a detailed medical research site that concludes that cancer of the penis is related to cigarette smoking! Check it out for yourself at;

www.cirp.org/library/disease/cancer/hellberg1/

If only I had known that when I was sixteen. Knowing how I felt about my new 'best friend' I'm sure I would have never started smoking. I think one of the best ways to stop a young guy from smoking would be to make sure he knew the information contained at that website. They may have a cavalier attitude about their lungs and their heart but they would not be too willing to put their 'reason for living' in such jeopardy. And I'm sure they'd hate anybody who would try and talk them into doing something like that.

At another site called; *The Truth* I found a lot of information and statistics that both alarmed and angered me. That kind of information helped me build my resolve to get out of the grips of these evil, lying "business" people at the cigarette companies, and to look with disdain and scorn at the advertising companies and the politicians who have constantly and knowingly deceived us over the years.

Fellow smokers, we have been played like a violin. They didn't just screw us out of our money. They screwed us out of our health, maybe our dicks and ultimately our lives.

In 1997, Barbara Amiel, the wife of Conrad Black, wrote; *"I don't think there is anything as hypocritical - criminal even - in our society as our tobacco policies. They make ordinary corruption look like child's play."*

Boy, am I surprised.
Afraid?
Yes. And outraged as well.

Calculate your risks

In March of 2003, the Memorial Sloan-Kettering Cancer Center in Manhattan, announced that a cancer-risk detection survey was available for smokers to assess their risk of contracting lung cancer from smoking. I went to their website and did the test. I gave them data that showed that I had not quit smoking.

Their test said that if I did not smoke another cigarette my risk of contracting lung cancer was 4%. If I continued to smoke, the risk was 7%.

Then I gave them the data that said I had quit three years ago. My lung cancer risk was still the same. 4%

Now, here's the interesting point. I then entered data that said I had quit seven years ago. My risk of contracting lung cancer was only 2%. I will be in that category in four years.

Try it for yourself at: www.mskcc.org

Here's what they say about the long term benefits you will enjoy when you quit.

"People who quit smoking live longer than those who continue to smoke. After 10 to 15 years, a previous tobacco user's risk of premature death approaches that of a person who has never smoked. About 10 years after quitting, an ex-smoker's risk of dying from lung cancer is 30 percent to 50 percent less than the risk for those who continue to smoke. Women who stop smoking before becoming pregnant or who quit in the first 3 months of pregnancy can reverse the risk of low birth weight for the baby and reduce other pregnancy-associated risks.

Quitting also reduces the risk of other smoking-related diseases, including heart disease and chronic lung disease.

There are also many benefits to smoking cessation for people who are sick or who have already developed cancer. Smoking cessation reduces the risk for developing infections, such as pneumonia, which often causes death in patients with other existing diseases."

When asked what age would be best to quit:

"Smoking cessation benefits men and women at any age. Some older adults may not perceive the benefits of quitting smoking; however, smokers who quit before age 50 have half the risk of dying in the next 16 years compared with people who continue to smoke. By age 64, their overall chance of dying is similar to that of people the same age who have never smoked. Older adults who quit smoking also have a reduced risk of dying from coronary heart disease and lung cancer. Additional, immediate benefits (such as improved circulation, and increased energy and breathing capacity) are other good reasons for older adults to become smoke free."

My take on that is that the very best time to quit is:

NOW!

CHAPTER 6
Watch "The Insider"

My appointment was for Wednesday, June 6ᵗʰ, at twelve-thirty. The night before I went, I watched the movie, 'The Insider.' I urge anyone who smokes to watch this movie. Besides giving you a whack on the side of the head, **it will fuel your anger toward the people you give your smoking money to.** (*'The people'* being the government *and* the tobacco industry.)

The part that really got to me was when Russell Crowe's character, Jeffrey Wigand stated;

"We are in the nicotine delivery business."

That hit me right between the eyes. That is the real mission statement for those nice people who present Marlboro, Winston, Players, Philip Morris, Virginia Slims, Joe Camel and Rothmans as merely a relaxing, refreshing pause in the day. They are, in fact just promoting a method of 'nicotine delivery.'

In the world of politics, advertising and public relations, it's called a *'spin.'* I visualized the spin-doctors sitting around their brainstorming table. *"We don't want them to see that they are killing themselves. We want them to see how cool they are. Winners. Part of the 'in' crowd. Yeah. That's it baby. The suckers love that stuff."*

And I was one of their best customers. A forty-year man. Just like 'The Duke.'

It really made me angry when Wigand stated that **the cigarette companies were actually exploring ways of making cigarettes more addictive.**

Addiction-enhancing research! Now there's a field of study I haven't seen advertised in university yet.

Digging deeper, I found that ammonia is one of the more than 599 ingredients that tobacco companies can and do mix and match at will. Anyway they want to. **Ammonia in a** cigarette makes your brain absorb more nicotine than it normally would.

Then they add licorice and cocoa, which sound innocent when you first hear about them, *except* that when you burn them, they act as **bronchodilators.** They dilate the bronchial tubes so that you expose more of the surface area of your lungs to come in contact with the smoke and thus ingest even more of the deadly substances (such as benzene, formaldehyde, hydrogen cyanide, carbon monoxide and tar) into your system. The 'hit' is bigger.

The addiction deepens.

Remember Richard Pryor? He's the comedian who set himself on fire by trying to '**freebase**' cocaine. You heat the coke up and turn it into a gas then inhale it. It gets you higher.

You are not going to believe this!

Scientists at the Oregon Health and Science University in Portland Oregon have detected 'free-base' nicotine in cigarettes. They are even able to quantify it.

Free-base nicotine, or gaseous nicotine is more quickly absorbed into the lungs and carried through the bloodstream into your brain. The hit is purer and gets there faster. Professor James Pankow reported in the journal, Chemical Research in Toxicology, "We found big differences in the percentages of freebase nicotine among 11 cigarette brands."

Gaseous nicotine is known to deposit super-quickly in the lungs and from there is transported super-quickly to the brain. The 'hit' gets there faster. Talk about an age of instant gratification.

Pankow went on to say, "Since scientists have shown that a drug becomes more addictive when it is delivered to the brain more rapidly, freebase nicotine levels in cigarette smoke thus are at the heart of the controversy regarding the tobacco industry's use of additives like ammonia and urea, as well as blending choices in cigarette design."

Now **this will really freak you out.** In 1997, Professor Pankow led a study which linked ammonia additives to increased freebase nicotine levels in cigarettes. Separate measurements were made of the first three puffs and then about eight subsequent puffs. In many cases, the freebase content was higher in the first puffs. Marlboro, for instance, had a freebase nicotine level of 0.6% in the first three puffs and 0.27% in later puffs.

Marlboro is quite high in freebase nicotine. They contain up to 9.6% in total. But, if you really want a freebase nicotine hit, try **American Spirit.** They offer you 36%. More hit for your smoking dollar. Better value.

Here's why it's legal. Freebase nicotine is generated by the additives but it is *not* in and of itself, an additive. So the tobacco guys can say, "No way! We would never put freebase nicotine in our cigarettes!" And they don't.

They just put the stuff in there that makes it all happen. But they never even mention that in their PR briefs.

"We will get you higher for less money."

I'd love to see their PR people give a press release saying something like, "Now don't worry about the freebase nicotine thing. We are not trying to kill you sooner. All we are trying to do with the freebase thing is make it tougher for you to quit. That way we can keep you in the revenue stream longer. No matter how high the government raises the price, you'll never be able to quit because we've got you so badly hooked. It's really just a sort of profit maximization thing that the suits in accounting dreamed up. So don't be getting all paranoid on us here. You can trust us."

It is illegal for you to buy benzene, formaldehyde and hydrogen cyanide in a store because they're considered to be hazardous chemicals. **But Benson and Hedges and their** partners in crime, will sell it to you as long as you use it to kill yourself and your friends and don't forget, your family.

Nicotine as a stand-alone drug is not what will kill you. It is not a carcinogen and that's why they don't ban it. Today however, there is some research which says that nicotine *sets the stage* for cancer.

It's all the other "flavour-enhancing" sustances that are added to the "product", which in truth, actually deepen your addiction.

Imagine that. They put stuff in the cigarette to deepen or enhance the addiction and the PR people turn it into some flavor hype. A *"new and improved"* type of thing.

The big advantage of the nicotine from the corporate point of view is that it's addictive. A lot of the other additives are just there to kick the addiction up a notch or two. (or as Emeril so eloquently puts it, *"Bam!"*)

In a 1993 British American Tobacco memo, the question was asked: *"Would disclosure of urea as a tobacco additive have a negative effect on consumer perception given that it is a constituent of urine?"*

The answer could well have been: *"No way. That's ridiculous. Don't forget now, these people are stupid. They smoke. We've got them hooked. They don't care what's in them. If they did they wouldn't be doing it in the first place. Besides, we've even got them convinced that it's cool. Are we good or what?"*

I thought to myself, "You dirty * * * * * * * *!" I'll bet you're even having similar thoughts right now. If not, you must work for a tobacco company or worse yet, you're a politician. In which case your thoughts about me are probably something like; "You rat! You've finally uncovered the truth and now you're trying to burst our golden bubble."

I watched a tobacco company guy on TV recently when he was interviewed by the press, after his company sued the Province of Saskatchewan for passing a law that forced cigarette retailers to put the cigarettes out of sight of the customers. You have to ask for the specific brand and size and they go into a little back room and get the product for you. (A rare incident where it seems that the government is not acting on behalf of the tobacco industry.)

The tobacco company executive claimed that they have a *constitutionally guaranteed right* to market their products in full view of the very people they are trying to enslave and they are going to fight for their rights. They just want a level playing field. They merely want to display their products to our children along side the Gatorade and The National Enquirer.

"After all man, it's a free country. We just want our right to lie and misrepresent our product to the public, protected. After all, we are people too."

After I saw that, I said to myself, "It probably would not be the dumbest idea I've ever had to buy some R.J. Reynolds stock. These people will stop at nothing to make money."

Then I figured, "**Imagine getting a dividend check from a company whose product killed your child or your parents or a good friend.**"

Or You.

What would you buy with that money?

Cuban cigars? Shares of R.J. Reynolds?

Did you know that R.J. Reynolds Sr., the guy who founded the R.J. Reynolds tobacco company died of pancreatic cancer? Old R.J. was instrumental in developing the cigarette in the first place. Before that, it was all pipes, plugs of chewing tobacco and cigars. They say he got his cancer from chewing tobacco. His son, R.J. Reynolds Jr. died from lung cancer. Read the family history and you'll se a family littered with smoking-related deaths.

Patrick Reynolds, the great grandson of R.J. Reynolds is the founder of; **The Foundation For A Smoke-Free America.**

An Organization devoted to eliminating the industry that his family instituted.

www.tobaccofree.com

Other illuminating Websites:

1: www.jeffreywigand.com
2: www.matrixths.com
3: www.fhcrc.org
4: www.quitsmoking.com

Who's your real friend?

I've seen the tobacco company executives say in countless interviews that they have found no really conclusive proof that cigarette smoking is harmful. Check the web sites and you'll see countless examples of tobacco company executives **lying through their tobacco stained teeth. Jeffrey Wigand has a great tape of seven of them doing it on national TV at his website. It's called the "Waxman Hearings."**

It would be nice to see somebody take the question to the next level. "Sir, you have testified here before this committee under solemn oath, that you have no conclusive proof that nicotine is addictive. Would you then say that if you did have proof that it was addictive, that you would then feel honor bound to dismantle your company and apologize to your customers for the big mistake?"

I can just see the guy squirming in his chair, "Yeah. Sure. Honest we would."

The U.S. Government's Department Of Justice has initiated a lawsuit against the big tobacco companies. It seeks to recover tobacco-related costs incurred by the U.S. government because of the tobacco company's many wrongful and illegal acts that increased the number of U.S. smokers and reduced the numbers that quit – thereby increasing the overall amount of tobacco-caused disease and related costs.

Now, here we have a government that gets a lot of money from the tobacco industry through taxes, and both sides acknowledge that crimes have been and are being committed, yet the company and in fact the industry that does this is allowed to survive and prosper. With health care costs going through the roof don't you think that at the very least the tobacco industry should pay their fair share of the damage they have caused... and are still causing?

Our governments know what this industry is doing and they allow this insanity to prevail. Why?

Money? Lots and lots of money. Money that gets politicians elected. Money that keeps lawyers in court. Money that gets judges appointed.

As my ole grandpappy used to tell me, "Son, if it looks like shit and smells like shit, you don't have to eat it to know that it is."

Folks, the *Pepsi* generation was really in fact the *Bullshit* generation. And I was a full-fledged, card-carrying, flag-waving, Marlboro smoking, Pepsi-drinking, establishment-loving member. The infuriating part is that they now want to recruit my kids to join. They want to recruit your kids to join as well.

I don't think so!

- There are an estimated 4,500,000 children and adolescents in the U.S.A. who smoke.

- Every day, 6,000 people under the age of 18 are "recruited" to try their first cigarette.

Q: Are you getting the feeling that the tobacco industry's marketing plan is working?

Surely you can't feel that the fact that so many young people are smoking is a nightmare for the tobacco company. They are not losing any sleep or spending money to try and get young people not to smoke. Ever see any ads that say:

"Wait until you're nineteen."

CHAPTER 7
The Last Mile

At 10 a.m. June 6th, 2000, I got in my car and headed for Windsor. During the seventy mile drive, I tried very hard to smoke a whole package of cigarettes. I figured that the *'hit'* would have to last me for the rest of my life.

So far. So good.

A most unforgettable moment occurred along the way when I stopped at a *Tim Hortons* coffee shop. For you Americans, *Tim Hortons* is the *Starbucks* of Canada. It was started by an old Toronto Maple Leaf hockey player and is now owned by *Wendy's* in the US. If you don't have a *Tim Hortons* near you, just wait, they're coming.

In politically correct Canada, some *Tim Hortons* coffee shops have a smoker's cage. That's a glassed-in room, where customers who smoke, are banished to perform their heinous deed and thus not befoul the politically correct.

It's okay for the smokers to take their kids in there though. I'm sure it helps get their lungs used to it so that when they smoke their first cigarette it won't be so difficult to inhale. **Their loving parents are preparing them well for their future addiction.**

As I walked by the 'cage' I glanced in at the smokers. There were eight of them in there. Smoking and drinking coffee.

Two of them were dragging these cute, little oxygen tanks behind them and taking oxygen straight into their nostrils through little hoses that they had clipped to their septum's.

They were also smoking cigarettes!

One hand would remove the oxygen tube from their nose. With the other, they'd take a drag. Then they would put the hose back in as they exhaled! Of course the oxygen was shut off. They just needed it so bad they never went anywhere without it and yet they still smoked.

I thought to myself, '*Whoaaaa. Now that's bad. This can never happen to me. This **will** never happen to me!*'

It made me recall a scene from 'Dawn Of The Dead.' Grey complexions. Sunken eyes. Very unhealthy looking. Resigned to a horrible fate. Not happy.

But with decent coffee and doughnuts.

Replaying that grim scene over and over in my mind became my final motivation as I puffed away and drove the remaining miles to Windsor and my salvation.

The moment of truth?

I parked my car at twelve fifteen. With only 15 minutes of smoking time left, I sat on the steps of the building and '*did*' my last cigarette. Actually my last three. I flicked the third butt into the gutter, and as I looked at it and prepared to step on it, the voice deep down inside me asked, *"Is that really the last one?"*

It dawned on me that I was afraid to commit to the idea of quitting forever because I didn't want to experience that feeling of disappointment in myself when I rationalized lighting up another cigarette later that day, after the treatment. **I was looking for a fall-back position so that I could justify the usual relapse.** It was a familiar feeling. I'd been here before… Many times.

Then the scene from the smokers' cage at *Tim Hortons* drifted through my mind. **Also** the fact that I was about to spend three hundred and twenty five after tax dollars!

I snarled and stomped on the cigarette. *"Don't be stupid. That's it! It ends now! Your kids and all your friends will know you for the schmuck that you are if you don't end this right here, right now. Plus you're going to blow three hundred and twenty five big ones. The suits at the tobacco companies will laugh all the way to the bank if you ever light one up again."*

Something wonderful happened right then and there. Faces of people....friends, relatives and famous people, who had all been slaughtered by this terrible habit came into my mind's eye. **They were nodding their heads in approval and smiling at me as if they knew that I had finally seen the light.** I didn't really see them. But I felt like they were there and in my mind's eye, I did see them. I still do. Others have told me the same thing. You may see it too.

At that particular moment, it all came together. Fear, anger, logic and finally, a surge of self respect. I was not going to be the mindless, predictable putz that I had been and they thought I still was, anymore.

I knew it was over. All I had to do now was go in there and do this thing. I was now a very determined man. I could visualize the suits at the tobacco companies throwing their cigarette butts down in disgust as they realized they were about to lose another customer. "Rats!"

With my fresh resolve, I went inside and took an elevator up to a small studio on the third floor. Looked kind of like a doctor's office. The receptionist checked me in, took my three hundred and twenty five after-tax, *you can not write them off* Canadian dollars.

Next, she gave me a form to read, fill out and then sign. This form basically guaranteed the laser people full immunity from any prosecution if their therapy didn't take. Their lawyers were trying to stay one step ahead of my lawyers.

Then a nice, young lady named Jody came out and invited me inside to a small room with what looked like a doctor's examining table, contorted into some sort of weird-looking Lazy Boy chair.

She beckoned me to get on it and lay back.

"Relax."

I didn't see any stirrups or anything else that might cause me any pain, so I put myself in Jody's seemingly capable hands and lay down on it.

"Please be gentle," I begged and my journey back to the light side of the force began.

Endorphins & Habits

Jody began the process by telling me what happened to me physiologically when I smoked, and this is basically what she said: "When you inhale a cigarette, you take an evil, and highly addictive drug called nicotine into your system. The cigarette is essentially just the vehicle that delivers the nicotine."

Just like The Insider guy said. So far everything adds up.

"Once inside your system, that lousy, rotten, little, dirtbag Mr. Nicotine tells your brain to release some endorphins into your system."

Jody continued, "Endorphins. They make you feel good. Real good. Better with than without."

Think about it now. Imagine drinking a cup of coffee and taking a drag on your favorite brand of cigarette after a nice, big dinner. A long, slow drag.

Okay. Inhale now.

That's it. Get all you can.

Now, suck it right down deep inside. All the way.

Feel that hit on your lungs? The nice little 'rush' in your brain? Soak it all in.

Hold it in. Enjoy the buzz. Feels good eh?

Okay now. Exhale.

Aaaaaggghhh. 'Oh man! That feels sooo good.'

Well sir. **That good feeling, that little '*rush*' you felt, that would be the endorphins kicking in.** You see, when you feel that urge for a cigarette it's not your craving for nicotine as such. It's really your system asking, no wait, it's begging, 'Come on. I want an endorphin hit. Right now! Please.'

Your brain says, 'Uh Uh. You didn't earn it. No way.' **But you don't want to earn the right to the endorphin hit. You just want the hit and you want it right now.** Besides, you know an easy way to get it. You light up a smoke. In so doing, you deliver Mr. Nicotine to what is now left of your brain.

He issues an order to your brain. An order your brain is powerless to refuse. *'Okay, give the little suck his endorphins. We'll make him feel good for a few minutes while we send a whole bunch of other crap into his system that'll really screw him up.'*

Did you ever notice that right after strenuous physical exercise you don't feel the urge to smoke? Well that's because your body is already getting an endorphin hit from your very own pre-programmed, regulatory system. You've heard of the 'runner's high?' That's what that is. The brain automatically injects those hard-earned, 'feel-good' endorphins into your system as a reward for your excellent efforts."

Jody continued, "**Now I'm going to use this little laser pen to stimulate certain areas of your nervous system so that you will enjoy a systematic and continuous release of endorphins into your system.** The dosage level will gradually decrease over the next twenty-eight days.

During that time your nicotine-addicted system will not need to be seeking any externally administered nicotine to trip the endorphin release mechanism since the endorphin release mechanism is going to be triggered internally, thanks to this treatment.

You see the **nicotine, in and of itself, is not really harmful. It's addictive but it won't give you cancer. It's all the other stuff mixed in with it that gives you the cancer, the heart diseases and other ailments.** Your brain doesn't know where the stimulus is coming from. It just knows that it is coming. You see, **it's the endorphin hit you're addicted to.** Thirty days from now that addiction will have faded away. Now what you have to do is work on **breaking the habit.**"

Major point here folks.

It's the endorphin hit you're addicted to. Not the nicotine. Find another way to get the endorphin hit and your only desire for a cigarette will be force of habit.

It all made sense to me. When I had lots of endorphins running through me I didn't crave nicotine. I picked up a cigarette out of habit. Those are the ones you don't enjoy. The reason is that you don't need them, (endorphin-ically speaking Nyuk! Nyuk!).

You are just feeding a habit, not an addiction. If I had endorphins being released inside my system from internally generated means, (i.e. laughter, exercise, a general feeling of confidence, sex etc.) I didn't need a cigarette **even though I automatically reached for one out of habit.**

I felt good seeing it in that light. The laser treatment would help me beat the addiction by taking care of the endorphin hits leaving me free to work on the habit. But with no addiction pulling at me, the habit would now be a lot easier to beat since I wasn't going nuts for an endorphin hit. I had lots of endorphins coursing through my veins due to her laser stimulations. I felt good. Still do.

Exactly what is a habit anyway?

A **habit** is an acquired effect of repeated acts. It is an inclination or an aptitude to act.

You repeat a certain activity, you get a habit. Therefore if you repeat 'not' doing the same activity you break the habit. A smoking 'habit' can be broken by simply *not* doing it twenty to thirty times.

Crack cocaine they say can be an addiction after one hit. But that doesn't make it a habit. Cigarettes take a little longer for the addiction to set in but they're even tougher to get off than crack. **One of the reasons for that is the habit aspect. If the**

addiction isn't prompting you to smoke, the habit is. I think that's because, **the more times you have to do it to establish the habit, the more times you have to 'not' do it in order to get off it.** I speak only from my own personal experience but I trust that knowledge more than most of the psycho-babble that I read.

This I'm sure is not rocket science, but when it was put before me that way by Jody, it helped me to understand what I had to do to conquer the demons. Right from the beginning, it looked simple. 'Don't do it' twenty to thirty times and the habit goes away. Upon sharing my experience, I have found it to be one that many others share with me.

If you do something twenty to thirty times, e.g. have a cup of coffee and light one up, you've pretty much got yourself a full-blown habit. You will now be prone to a habitual urge to light one up whenever you have a coffee. The addiction gets fed but now you're also feeding it out of habit. That's even worse.

Words to live by:
Habits are easy to acquire and tough to get rid of.

Jody continued, "It's a very slippery slope when you combine addictive substances with non-addictive habitual rituals like drinking coffee, or booze, or driving, or before you go to sleep or as soon as you wake up."

"Or after sex?"

"Now you've got it. Do it twenty to thirty times and you've got a habit. But, by the same token, *don't* do it twenty to thirty times and you've broken the habit. The habitual urge eventually goes away."

That's the theory anyway. The numbers may vary according to your physiological and psychological makeup but unless you are a certifiable section eight, I believe the theory is basically correct.

She continued, "So, in the next twenty to thirty days, you merely change your daily routines to avoid and thereby

eliminate the habitual smoking urges while at the same time, with this treatment, you are being weaned of your physical addiction. Pretty cool eh?"

I had to agree.

She spent the next twenty minutes running this laser pen in between my fingers, on the inside of my wrist, up my arm, in my ears and then down the other arm and in between the fingers. I assume those are all the places where my nervous system comes in close contact with the surface of my not-so-nervous system. There was no pain whatsoever. Just a little tingle.

As she did this, she told me a lot of helpful things I could do to help eliminate the urges due to my habit over the next thirty to sixty days.

- **Drink lots of water.** You will be detoxifying your system. Flushing the poisons out.
- **Go for walks. Ride a bike.** You are in a recovery phase and you need to give yourself a break.
- **Do not hang around with people who smoke.**

> I thought of Dom Irerra's great bit.
> "Do you mind if I smoke?"
> "Not really. Do you mind if I fart?"

The key was to change my daily routines. **Mess up the habit demons.** They hate that. Get my system used to a new and different schedule so that it wouldn't miss the cigarettes.

You don't want your system to say, 'Hey there. We're having a coffee aren't we? Well then, hello! Where's our cigarette?'

Instead, you want your system to be involved in the walk, or the bike ride and the long, frequent, system-cleansing and detoxifying drinks of water so that it doesn't miss the cigarettes. **You are actually implanting new habits.** Good habits.

When you think about it, replacing old bad habits with new good habits isn't such a bad idea. **Young people won't see this as plainly as we older folks who, thanks to the smoking habits of our friends and ourselves have had more than one mortality crisis.** We finally start to see the light at the end of the tunnel and figure, "Why rush it? Let's try and lengthen the tunnel a little."

The kids figure, "It's a long way off. I'll worry about it later." (At this point, I would caution the guys who do this to remember that thing about the penis cancer.)

How do I know we procrastinate? Simple. I did it. Remember now, I did not know about the penis cancer thing.

Do not rationalize your smoking by using me as an example. The fact that I survived it is foreshadowed by the fact that I still have at least four more years to sweat it out before I'm out of the woods. Believe me, you do not want to do that.

Finally the nice lady smiled and said, "Okay. That's it. We're finished. By the way, if you want to come back for a free booster in the next sixty days you may do so. But not if you are still smoking."

"Well thank y'a baby. Thank y'a vurrry much."

CHAPTER 9

Free At Last! Free at Last! Thank God Almighty, I'm Free At Last!

At 1:30 p.m., I was back in my car. **A non-smoker.** I remember walking through the lobby and throwing my pack of smokes into a garbage pail. I was scared, but deep down inside I had a good feeling. I knew way down in the cockles of my heart that this time it was going to work.

It was over. I believed! **I was free!**

I felt like jumping up in the air and clicking my heels together.

The period I feared the most was the first twenty-four hours. Due to the fact that it had been **over fifteen years since I had gone a full day without a cigarette,** this most significant hurdle would be a personal moral victory of immense value.

I had been weak. But, now I felt strong. I now believed!

The laser treatment, the scene from "The Insider," which fueled my rage towards the "Nictotine-Delivery' industry, and the macabre image of the people in 'the cage' at the *Tim Hortons* combined to give me a newfound strength.

The first day? No problem. I spent the afternoon with my old friend Woodrow. We went for a long drive through the countryside.

We have been friends for over thirty years. He was a smoker when we first met and had quit twenty years ago. He went to a hypnosis seminar. Walked in as a pack-a-day smoker. Did a twenty minute hypnosis session and walked out a non-smoker. **Has never had one since.** "Don't want'em. Don't need'em."

I think it was so easy for him because he's basically a very weak-minded individual. Open to the power of suggestion. Horror movies scare the daylights out of him. I mean, the guy freaked out watching "The Shining." But like they say, "Whatever works."

He took me out for dinner and afterward, we went to a Casino. Lots of smokers in there. No problem with any urges whatsoever. I almost psyched myself out. Wondering when the urge would come. Afraid I would cave in when it did.

But the 'scenes' kept playing over in my mind. Something inside my head kept coming up that said, "Nope. It's over. You're free of it." Must have been those laser-induced endorphins that Jody gave me.

As the day wore on, I started to feel better because I realized I wasn't going nuts for a smoke. I kept feeling better and better as the time passed. It's like my inner self was acting all on its own. Beating back any semblance of an urge that surfaced. My weak outer self was not being asked to deal with it. Something inside me was doing it.

Jody's words kept playing over and over in my head. My attitude progressed from that of a motivated, gung-ho guy to a quite serenity that comes only with self-confidence.

My newfound belief in myself was paying off. Bigtime. The tobacco industry was in big trouble and the government had just lost a very reliable source of revenue.

Once you get through the first day, your belief that you can do it will be strengthened. **Each hour I grew stronger and happier with the realization that it was over.** I really believed I was beating it. And you know what they say, "If you believe you can or you can't, you're probably right." You may get a little sick of that but it's a huge point.

That belief felt good. I knew I had it further behind me every time the thought came to my mind. The momentum just kept building.

Each day I grew stronger.

The first week? No problem.

Sure, I had a few habitual urges. But they were fleeting. They came upon me at times when I would normally have a cigarette. But **I was so damned proud of myself for making it as far as I had, that I knew I wouldn't cave in.**

I would momentarily have the urge. Then something inside me would say, "No! Remember? You quit. You've gotten over the major hurdles. You're free of it!"

I can only call it a 'rush.' That good feeling that comes over you when you achieve a milestone.

You wait and see. It will happen for you too!

If the urge is strong, just say to yourself, "I'll have a glass of water and wait ten minutes. If I still feel like having one then, maybe I'll do it."

Next thing you'll notice its a few hours later and you haven't even thought about it. **You feel better each and every time you make it through one of those episodes.**

You look back and feel glad that you made it through the last one and realize, "That wasn't so bad." Each time it will get easier.

If you're like me, and it's been a long time since you went a full day without a puff, then, once you make it through the first day, you will experience a huge psychological lift. You start to really believe. You now know you can do it.

Whenever I thought about having a smoke it was always, "Nope. Never again. Not just today. Never a-frigging-gain!"

The addiction urge never did come. It was just the 'habit' urge.

After dinner, when I had a beer, after I had sex, before I had sex. Not however, during.

Whenever the urge did come, I would always say to myself, *"Nope. I've quit. I've made it out of that swamp and I ain't a goin' back in there. Besides, I'm not going to give one more dime of my hard-earned money to those nicotine-delivery, addiction-enhancing corporate dorks at the cigarette company."*

I also didn't feel any sudden bursts of patriotism to replenish the lost revenue for my various beloved governments.

With those thoughts and feelings to motivate and empower me, the urge left quickly. **My mindset came through for me. It still does.**

Each day, the incremental gain in personal pride you will feel for getting through this process will strengthen you. **You will smile at the weakened habitual urges as they fade away in your memory.**

I still drink coffee. But somehow even bad coffee tastes better. Smoking will now be something you used to do back in the old days when you were weak and stupid.

The first year? No problem.

The first three years? No problem.

The rest of my life which is now hopefully a little further away? No problem.

The rapture is upon me.

I am enlightened. I've beaten it. And that feels good. Real good.

Perhaps that thrill of victory over the demon weed and its evil promoters and scumbag benefactors is the best feeling of all.

My dad smoked.

For a long time. From the start of World War II until after the Vietnam War.

He quit cold turkey. If you were to ask him what personal life-accomplishment he is most proud of, he'd probably tell you; **"It was definitely quitting smoking. Of all the things I have ever done, by far and away my proudest accomplishment is that I was finally able to quit smoking and stay off the damned things.**

Oh yes, I was also the captain of a Corvette in the Royal Canadian Navy and froze my ass off in the north Atlantic for five long years during World War II, on the prowl for shithead Nazis in U Boat 571 and the like.

And I did sail my own boat from Canada all the way down to Grenada. And back. Twice. But looking back on it all, I believe it was actually much, much tougher to quit smoking."

Vegas: The Ultimate Test.

A few months later, in Las Vegas, after a big night at the tables, I got a real big urge for, "Just one. Come on man. Celebrate. You're a winner. You can handle it. See if it still tastes as great as it used to."

Then the little voice said to me, *"Do you really want to go through all this bullshit and spend all that money and still wind up smoking?"*

That did it.

The mindset kicked in.

And stayed in.

I got drunk instead.

The next morning I remember thinking to myself that; *"It was pretty smart of me not to have had a cigarette last night, because any of the endorphin-induced effects I might have enjoyed then, would be long gone by now. And I'd have a whole new set of problems to deal with this morning. Along with this hangover."*

Oh yeah.

I quit drinking that day.

For a while anyway.

Weight Watchers.

People (mostly women) ask me about weight. As in, did I gain any?

After seven months, I was even. Which was about 15 pounds over my fighting weight.

After ten months I was up another seven pounds. But these days I drink a lot more water and now that I'm off the weed, I find myself doing things and eating things that are better for my health. I'm also only five pounds over my fighting weight.

I didn't worry too much about staying healthy when I was smoking because I figured, **"What's the point? The cigarettes are probably gonna kill me anyway."**

It's sort of like the guy who goes to MacDonalds' and orders a quarter-pounder with double cheese, fries and then tops it off with a *Diet Coke*. I could be missing something there but I have to ask myself, *"What's the point?"*

Let's face it. Smoking is a death-wish. You can't suck and blow at the same time. If you want to be healthy, don't smoke. **Getting a healthy body and a healthy heart is the least of your problems if you smoke.** There is no point in worrying about anything else if you smoke. Except maybe going to prison. But then, they do allow smoking in prison.

The point is, **once I quit, I started to believe that I could live longer.** And in a better way. The death-wish was gone.

Replaced by an overpowering urge to live. Long and well. I felt the same way after I got my divorce.

Ask anybody who's kicked the habit. They'll tell you that this urge to live long and well is a delightful little by-product.

As Time Goes By:

I am now in my fiftieth smoke-free month. Over fifteen hundred days. Without even one lousy, rotten, stinking little puff. Only 5 pounds over my fighting weight and headed in the right direction. It may sound wierd, but **I am determined to die the absolute picture of good health.**

The biggest shock I got was when I did the math and realized that **in the last three years since I quit, I have *'not spent'* over $9,600 after-tax dollars and *'not smoked'* over 36,000 cigarettes.** The idea that I would have smoked 36,000 more cigarettes if I hadn't quit when I did, was shocking. I can't believe that I'm not a long way out of the woods having just missed those thirty six thousand smokes alone.

When people who smoke ask me about quitting, they are amazed to realize how many cigarettes they have smoked and how much money they have spent on their smoking habit, just since I quit.

People, mainly smokers and ex-smokers often ask me. "Do you miss it?"

I tell them. Honestly. "No I do not."

At the *News Cafe* in South Beach, Miami, I asked a lady at the table beside me, who was smoking, "Does that thing taste as good as it smells?"

She smiled elegantly and said in a rich, Corinthian accent, "Why yes it certainly does. May I offer you one?"

With a smile, "No thanks. I quit."

"Really. Congratulations. How long has it been?"

"Six months."

"Six months! You lucky bastard!"

And this lady was a nun!

You are not going to believe this:

I understand that there are smoker's rights groups. Now just try to visualize what a meeting of people who care enough about the rights of the smoker to go to a meeting would be like. A few smokes shy of a pack I'd say. Fighting for their right to light up anywhere they want and to hell with the rest of us.

'The United Pro Choice Smokers Choice Newsletter,' invites you to join their ranks and take up the sword of justice. These people actually believe that there is some kind of weird conspiracy being perpetrated by the "Lasker Syndicate" (American Cancer Society, American Heart Association, American Lung Association, American Public Health Association, et al.), to deprive the American citizens of their basic, constitutionally guaranteed *'right'* to smoke.

In their January issue they had an article about Canada's 'Nazi-Style' war against smokers. They warn of a conspiracy by the 'nazi' style medical industry and the cancer society who make a big deal out of nothing. I mean all they want is for us not to waste money creating diseased people with cancer by smoking.

At the very least, we should be told the truth. If the tobacco industry would do at least that, then I am sure the four and a half million Americans under the age of eighteen who smoke would not have been quite so anxious to start smoking.

I agree that you have a right to smoke. You also have a right to jump of the Golden Gate Bridge. But I don't think they should have people opening a booth on the bridge giving lessons on how to do it.

I don't agree that the tobacco industry has a right to market the product using the techniques they do and they certainly don't have the right to buy the influence of the political system.

But they do! And they do it with your money!

I wonder where most of the funding for the smoker's rights web sites and other publications comes from?

Duh!

Now here's the weird part; did you know that the American Civil Liberties Union actually provides some financial support for those groups!

Why?

Well, The American Civil Liberty Union gets financial support from the tobacco industry but doesn't actually like to boast about it, if you know what I mean.

They have to lay the money off somewhere so they support the smoker's rights groups with a few of their ill-gotten bucks since I guess they feel that smoking is at some level, a civil liberty that needs to be fought for by some poor, deluded putz.

It's what's known as:

"The Price Of Silence"

See, I told you, you wouldn't believe it.

Okay then: So, all I have to do now is call 1 800 807 8714, make an appointment, give them the $325 after-tax, no frigging way you can write them off Canadian dollars and it's all over. Right?

Sorry. I don't think it's quite that simple. Laser therapy doesn't work all by itself. In my opinion there are four major factors that combined with the 'process' to contribute to my successful quitting effort. None of them by themselves were able to get me through the process, but when all four of them merged, I did it with no problem. I was *"ready"* as they say.

The 'process' involved is this. By now, you will have decided that you really do want to quit. But, you are worried that you do not have the resolve to do it. You are afraid of spending some money and some time to do this and ending up still smoking. That's how I felt.

What you need to do first is this: **Relax.**

You aren't going to quit tomorrow. **All you have to do tomorrow is pick the day you are going to quit.** Usually about thirty to sixty days from tomorrow. When I called the Alpha Institute, they told me I could come in to see them on June 6th. This was in April. So by making the appointment, I set the date.

Then I had about sixty or so days to get my head in the right place to do this. I did not realize it at the time but **the events of the next sixty days set the stage for me to build and confirm my commitment to quit smoking.** When I walked in to my appointment it was over. I was angry, afraid and very aware that it was a dumb way to spend money that would kill me.

By just making the appointment I gained a huge feeling of relief in that I felt I had taken a very positive step toward my goal of quitting. Over the next sixty days, I would experience the four stages, described in the next chapter.

It was not a conscious movement. It just so happened that the movie, "The Insider" was released on DVD at the time. I also did the math, and then, out of curiosity, went and looked up some websites related to these issues. It just kind of took off from there.

I kept digging and getting angrier and more afraid as I went along. The numbers I came across are absolutely staggering. I took the ones that most impressed me and put them in this book. I'm sure that as you read on, you will experience the same gamut of emotions that I did since after all, **we are all victims of the same monsters.**

What follows are the four stages or factors that you need to go through between now and your quit date. **I mean really go** *through* **them. Don't just read about them.** *Experience* **them.**

Do that and I guarantee you that if you are not angry, afraid and logically motivated to a firm sense of resolve to quit smoking or better yet, never start, then you are really too stupid to live, let alone breed. Your death due to smoking will in a way, be deemed a cleansing of the gene pool.

Most guys don't mind being tagged 'a little crazy' but **we all hate being tagged as stupid.** It's tough stuff to take in, but you need to fully understand and believe in your heart of hearts that; **Smoking is dangerous, stupid and very expensive.** Don't kid yourself any longer with any of that crap about addictions or habits. Stop it. You have to or you are not going to be happy with what happens next.

The 4 Stages are:

1: Doing the math. All of the math

2: Being afraid. Very afraid.

3: Getting mad. Mad as hell.

4: Now, get some help.
   (Pills, patches, laser therapy, smoking cessation
   clinics, smoke-enders meetings, gum, hypnotism,
   acupuncture, whatever they come up with next.)

Whatever it takes.
If it helps it's good.

Congratulations!

You are now the tobacco industry's
worst nightmare.

You are a smoker
who's ready to quit!

Let's head for Stage 1

CHAPTER 10

Stage 1: Do *All* The Math

"Cigarettes are bad for you as an individual but they're good for the economy overall."

What's a body to do?

First: **Do the math. All of the math.**

Don't just figure out what a package of smokes costs and how much you are spending on your habit. Figure out what you have to do to get the money. How much of your time is really involved in getting that money and supporting your habit. **How much of your working life has already been devoted to this habit.** It's ridiculous when you think about all the money you have spent, all the taxes you had to pay in order to clear the money and then how much of your time was spent working to earn that money.

Then learn where all the money goes. How much it costs to make a package of cigarettes. How much do the tobacco companies get? How much do the various governments get? You will be amazed.

You will start to feel like a schmuck for ever being a part of this ridiculous industry. **You will see how their total disrespect for your intelligence is all a part of this.** You not only need a lot of money to smoke, you've got to be stupid. Once those feelings start to come out, you will be pretty far along the road.

The really 'smart' smokers economics-wise, are the ones who buy them from all the tax free/duty free outlets. They will have a lower cost per death index to proudly point to. *"If you are in the 50% tax bracket and you smoke, from a purely financial point of view, you are too stupid to live!"*

The Personal Math:

It costs a lot of money to smoke. From $7.60 a pack in Ontario to over $9.00 a pack in Alberta and Saskatchewan.

About four American dollars per pack in the USA, although I did see them for as low as $1.89 per pack in Nevada. Native Americans and Canadians have a thriving little mail order business going selling tax-free cigarettes.

One night before I quit, I fired up my computer and opened an Excel spreadsheet. Then I built a little table that helped me figure out how many cigarettes I have smoked since I first started, how much I have spent on them and how much money I had to earn in order to 'net' the money I needed to buy them.

What makes me feel really stupid is the realization that **over my forty year smoking career, I purchased and smoked 14,600 packs for a total of 365,000 cigarettes!**

And I inhaled every one of them!

To do that I had to earn over $60,000 after tax dollars! In total I earned over a hundred thousand dollars and paid forty of it in income taxes, just to get my hands on the sixty I needed to buy the damned cigarettes!

An interesting note. Assuming they don't raise the prices any higher than they are today, if you do what I did and smoke what I smoked, the smoking habit will cost you $117,000 of today's after-tax money.

Hold on now, here's the insane part:

The average Canadian must earn eleven dollars to purchase one pack of cigarettes. Here's the breakdown:

He pays three forty of it in income taxes leaving seven sixty, the price of a small pack.

The Provincial and Federal governments get $6.10 and the cigarette companies get a measly buck and a half.

In total, **you earn eleven dollars and give nine fifty to the government.** I've heard that they can make a package of cigarettes for less than a dime. This means that you have to earn eleven dollars to buy something that costs about a dime to make! And you have to do it every day! **I did it for forty years!**

Here's why we're schmucks:

Your government, the one you elected to look after the best interests of you and your family, collects its taxes, sits on its fat duff and throws peanuts at the anti-smoking people, while allowing large corporations to deceive and ultimately slaughter its customers. **The tobacco industry has the only legally sold and controlled product in the world that actually kills its customers.**

And the citizens, (that's us, the schmucks and incidentally, the voters) let them get away with it. **We don't really** *do* **anything to stop it.** We can protest and we can ban it in public places but we will never stop it as long as there's a buck to be made by selling it

Are you in favor of capital punishment? If you are against capital punishment on humanitarian grounds, just watch a lung cancer patient go through the last week of their life. Personally, I'd rather be electrocuted.

Instead, we ban capital punishment and allow the tobacco industry to flourish.

More mixed messages for our kids eh?

Here's a guy who's not a schmuck.

In November, 2003, I was installing a home theater system in the home of a guy my age that I had known all my life.

During the course of the installation he asked me if I still smoked. He remembered me as a smoker from our high school days together.

After I told him that I had quit, I asked him if he still smoked. He told me that he had quit twenty seven years ago.

"The day my last kid was born."

"How'd you do it," I asked?

"Cold turkey."

"What was your motivation? Health?"

"Nope. The government raised the taxes on them and the price went from forty cents a pack to sixty five cents a pack. I figured screw it. I can't afford this. Besides, I hate paying taxes."

I laughed. I started to think about all the money he had saved over the years. Then I cried.

He must feel pretty good from having made such a smart financial decision so many years ago. The good health he enjoys today is a side benefit of that decision.

Isn't it?

More evidence of the wisdom of that decision is his brand new thirty five foot camper van.

Now, let's do some Industrial (albeit Non-Enron) Type Math:

In 1776, Adam Smith warned that the interests of the monied classes were not to be trusted to reflect the public interests. Historically, there has always been a conflict between the private interests of business and those of the public. That's why we have unions (and ultimately Communism). To protect the workers.

Free Trade is another interesting example of the other point of view. It protects the interests of big business. If the job costs too much at home, we get some other poorly paid guy in a country that doesn't have unions to make the product and ship it to us, the jobless people who used to work in the unions.

The business people want to make a buck and will stop at nothing to do so. The public has always tended to be a little too trustworthy but I think we are starting to get over that since we are all becoming increasingly aware of the fact that we are, as Norman Mailer so eloquently puts it, "swimming in bullshit." That doesn't seem to be the big secret today that it once was back in the heyday of the Duke, the original he-man 'Rock' and Bogie.

Yet people always seem to be able to put one over on us all.

Why?

Because when the bullshit is well presented, we basically want to believe it. In other words, we don't demand that it *not* be bullshit. Just that it be well-presented, attractive bullshit.

This is the thinking that built Las Vegas, Ottawa, Washington and Hollywood. It made Rock Hudson famous. Billy Crystal said it beautifully as Fernando Lamas, "It is more important to look good than it is to feel good."

What you see is not necessarily what it is.

Bullshit. It's what makes bingo parlors so prosperous. It's why we buy lottery tickets. We are told and therefore *believe* that there is an easy way to the big bucks. Every time I drive down the strip section of Las Vegas Boulevard I have to remind myself that it's my money I'm looking at, not Caesar's.

All that happens **when they figure we're on to them is that we get a new kind of bullshit.** The tobacco industry spends a lot of money inventing new types of bullshit to get around the stumbling blocks we erect for them. They ban the tobacco companies from advertising on TV and in magazines, so they come up with new ways of doing it.

For example, here is some information from a group in California who conducted an investigation called; *Operation Storefront*. It was sponsored by the *Youth Against Tobacco, Advertising and Promotion* who conducted a large survey of marketing practices in California to demonstrate how the tobacco industry spends $4 billion advertising dollars on storefront ads at your basic *7 Eleven* type convenience stores where our kids go almost every day. Did you ever see one of those places at noon hour?

Among the more striking, statistically significant, findings were the following:

1: An average of 25.26 tobacco ads per store!

2: Higher number of ads in stores within 1000 feet of schools

3: Higher number of exterior ads near schools

4: Significantly higher number of tobacco ads in stores that have tobacco ads next to candy

5: Significantly higher number of tobacco ads in stores that have tobacco ads placed below 3 feet (eye level for children).

6: More than half of the stores have no posted anti-smoking message (in violation of state law).

Now, if our kids go to those stores about nine or ten times a week, what do you think the message they're getting is?

By the age of sixteen the average kid has had over 75,000 advertising messages telling him to drink alcohol. Ever wonder why you read a lot these days about teenage drinking. We program them to do it.

I'd be willing to bet you that the average sixteen year old gets at least that many messages telling them to smoke. That's why, in the USA, 3,000 young people start smoking every day!

At a 3% success rate for quitting, only 90 of them will ever be able to quit for good. So you can now see what they are prepared to do in order to get their 2,910 new lifetime customers every frigging day of the week. Incidentally, **around seven hundred of those lifetime customers are in grade six.**

Just look at how smart we were. Historically we have shown that we will believe just about anything they tell us:

- Gambling is fun.
- Government is good for us. (But not to us)
- Buy this lottery ticket and become a millionaire. Everybody's doing it.
- Politicians always tell us the truth.
- Smoking is cool.
- We can all have a great body if we buy the latest no-actual work-needed, ab machine.
- If we wear all those clothes in those magazines and dye our hair all those colors, we can be beautiful people too. Just like Brad and Jennifer.

They essentially want us to believe that there is an easy road to the American dream. We don't need to work. Or think. Or exercise. No, all we have to do is buy the bullshit and everything will be okay.

One of these days we will eat a hamburger with a fine print label on it that says: "No actual food was used in the preparation of this product." (What I'm dying to hear is the hype they will use to try and convince us that that's good for us.)

In Canada in 2002, over forty three billion (43,000,000,000) cigarettes were purchased by five point seven million smokers. That's over forty one million dollars a day spent by Canadians on cigarettes. (That's one hundred and seventeen million and eight hundred thousand smokes per day which comes out to 20.8 cigarettes per day per smoker. Therefore the average Canadian smokes a pack a day. Just like me. That means the numbers are still in-line.)

The various governments take over thirty five million of that every day so you are forced to ask yourself if the government really wants us to quit. Again with the mixed messages.

In the US, about 25.9 million men (27.1 %) and 22.8 million women (22.2 %) smoke.

90% of them started before age 20; 50% started by age 14; (that's twenty four million smokers who have smoked ever since the age of 14) and 25% began smoking by age 12. That's grade 6 folks. (twelve million smokers who began smoking by the age of 12) Now I ask you. Is that a crime?

With 4.5 million teenage smokers in the USA... (12 through 17) it's easy to see how well the in-store marketing campaigns at the convenience stores are working.

Imagine that a million dollars a day was spent in advertising, trying to get us to use cocaine. Do you think we'd have a lot of coke-heads around?

Well folks, **in the USA they spend about a million an *hour* advertising and promoting cigarettes.** And it is working.

In Canada 200 young people take up smoking every day. A mere 3% of them will ever be able to quit and stay quit forever. (I am determined to stay in that 3% category.)

Let's see. Three percent of two hundred is six. So the tobacco industry in Canada gets a hundred and ninety four new lifetime clients each and every day.

Let's see now. The tobacco industry in Canada loses 45,000 customers per year to death from smoking-related causes and they replace them with seventy thousand, eight hundred and ten young people. Sounds to me like a net gain of 25,810 lifers per year.

Let's do this again now but break it down to a daily figure this time. Assuming 45,000 deaths per year in Canada, that means 123 people die every day. Yet 200 young people start smoking every day. My math says that each day, the tobacco industry in Canada gains 87 new customers!

Yet *they* tell us that the number of smokers is down. If that's true, it can only be because older people are kicking the habit. I hope so. But I don't think so. Remember. **The truth is very difficult to find.** They keep it well hidden.

Do you think they are actually ever going to come right out and say, "Okay, here are the numbers folks. The number of people who smoke. The number of people we kill and the number of people we entice on a daily basis into our web of treachery and deceit."

The cold hard math is the only thing you can believe.

Figure it out for yourself and you can only come to one conclusion. **They're killing us in larger numbers every day! You *have* to quit. We have to convince our kids that they can't even start!**

On a worldwide basis, WHO reports that based on current patterns of consumption, more than 500 million people who live on the planet today will die from tobacco. Today, tobacco kills around 3.5 million people a year. That number will rise to 10 million during the 2020s or the 2030s. 12% of all deaths will be caused by tobacco.

If you are a smoker today and you do not quit the Vegas odds are even money that you will be one of those numbers.

What the regulatory bodies really ignore is the basic marketing ploy of the tobacco industry. They know that traditional advertising will not make anybody smoke. All it does is motivate people to choose a certain brand. **The way to get people to start smoking is by urging them to, "C'mon. Try one. It's cool. You'll be cool too."**

Once they get you to do that their evil work is done. You continue smoking just as they know you will. You have been recruited.

They say that 'crack cocaine' is an addiction that takes hold after the first hit. Cigarettes don't take too much more than that and now that they are using 'free base' nicotine in them, the addiction takes hold even faster today than it used to.

The tobacco companies would rather be in the tobacco business than the cocaine business because they know that tobacco is a much tougher drug to quit than cocaine.

Relax now. The 'free base' aspect is there not because they are trying to kill you, they're just trying to make it tougher for you to quit. Isn't it frightening? **Smoking is something you really do not want to screw around with.**

Another major benefit of tobacco, from a marketing standpoint is that it takes so long to kill you. The tobacco companies (a.k.a. *Merchants of Death*) get a forty-year customer who drops a hundred large on his habit before he gets taken out. Therefore, for business *and* political reasons tobacco must be legalized.

Why?

Money!

This makes me think of the car companies and the oil and gas companies who get together and make sure that all of our cars run on oil and gas instead of say, water or even better, urine. Think of the old motto:

What's good for General Motors, is good for the USA?

I was brought up naively believing that a good company should provide its' customers with honest, accurate information about the products they're selling. This way people can make informed decisions about the products they spend their hard-earned money on. The bad product companies will fail and the good product companies will prosper.

The economy will work, the government will be honest, everything will be wonderful and we'll all go to heaven and find out who really killed J.F.K.

I know, I know. I'm dreaming. Right?

Nonetheless, with those ideals in mind, we should therefore insist that the tobacco industry tell us:

1: Smoke if you really want to, but according to the American Lung Association, 430,700 Americans (45,000 Canadians) are killed annually by smoking related diseases. These products that we sell you are actually killing about 1200 Americans (and 125 Canucks) every day! That's fifty an hour in the US and one every ten minutes in Canada! So go ahead and smoke if you want to. Schmuck!

2: In order to keep our stockholders happy the tobacco company must replace those 1200 (US) customers who die each day with at least 1200 new smokers just to maintain the customer base. And if we get a chance to grow the customer base, we owe it to our stockholders to do that.

Don't forget now, this is a business and we will do everything we can get away with and a lot of things that we can't get away with but can bribe our way through to get you. Watch out!

3: In our efforts to do this, we will shamelessly bullshit you and your kids about the harmful and deadly affects of the products we offer you. We will spend huge amounts of money to try and 'position' our products as a totally cool thing for you and your kids to do.

(**Remember this,** *the family that smokes together all die the same horrible death.* **If you don't believe that just look up the R.J. Reynolds family. They are dying proof of that statement.**)

4: And we will try to get you to believe that we are responsible business people. Again with the same technique. Bullshit.

5: We will lie to you and tell you that we are changing the blends of our tobacco in order to improve the taste, but in reality we are just manipulating the nicotine potency in order to boost sales by deepening your addiction to our products.

6: Furthermore, we will spend tons of the money you give us to back the political campaigns of politicians who will not vote in your best interests, but rather, will vote to let us have our way.

Don't be so selfish now and just be thinking of your own self. **Smoking may be bad for you but it is good for us.**

"But they're just kids!"

When you think about it, it just maximizes the productivity of the tobacco industry's marketing dollar to recruit young smokers.

1: They are easier to get since they have less concern about longevity and will be in the tobacco company's customer database for a longer period of time. Living proof of the old adage, *'Too bad that youth is wasted on young people.'*

2: Like all good capitalists the tobacco companies like to grow their market/profit numbers to satisfy their stockholders who are addicted to profit.

The government (remember now, this is only a dream) would then step in and say, "Hey. You can't kill the citizens that way. It's just not right fellas.

These people have elected us to act in their best interests so we are, at the very least, going to insist that you tell them the brutal truth about the shit you're selling them. We will no longer allow you to use your money to purchase our goodwill instead we will act for the good of the people who voted for us.

And another thing you guys, kindly knock it off with the John Wayne, Rock Hudson, Joe Camel shit."

Sorry folks. Not gonna happen. If you really want to know who, what and where; just follow the money. It leads to big business, the halls of justice and a lot of lawyers.

The why part is easy.

History's oldest and most common 'why.' Greed.

Good old fashioned greed.

Spelled ;

M – O – N – E – Y.

This'll really kill y'a:

In the USA, the Department of Health and Human Services estimates that 90 percent of smokers begin tobacco use before age 20. And today that number is around 3,000 people per day!

50% of smokers begin their habit by age 14; and 25% begin their addiction by age 12. That's the 6th grade folks!

Players please. The number one position in the cigarette world is owned by Philip Morris. They get 49% of the U.S. market. **They spent $350 million dollars in the 3rd quarter of 2002 to promote their brands to you.**

Number two in the business is R.J. Reynolds at 22.9%. They are aggressively going after Philip Morris customers and so the war is on.

Prizes and discounts are the bait.

You are the target.
You
and especially,

your kids.

Follow the money? Good idea.

Let's see just how big this tobacco business really is. The WHO (World Health Organization, a division of the United Nations) claims that the industry makes about $168 billion (U.S.) per year worldwide.

There are only thirty countries in the world whose GDP exceeds that number. Those profits are shared by the governments and the tobacco companies.

Now let's see who stands to lose if you quit?

1: The tobacco industry will lose a lot of money if you quit smoking. A forty year smoker is a hundred thousand dollar lifetime customer.

2: The medical industry and **the pharmaceutical industry** stand to lose a lot of money if you quit. *Hospital Practice*, a trade magazine, stated on 6/15/93 that smokers are admitted to hospitals twice as much as non-smokers. Think of all those hundred thousand-dollar cancer operations, the quadruple bypasses, the radiation chemotherapy, those ridiculously expensive drugs and those MRIs. That's money that you'll be depriving those poor people of by your selfish refusal to simply do your duty to the economy and continue smoking.

3: The government will lose big time. Provincial, state, municipal, federal. They're all in on it. Those people get pensions and perks that you won't begin to believe and it takes money to do that. Tons of it.

In the U.S.A. the average Federal government take alone, for the last seven years averages six billion dollars a year. That's over sixteen million dollars a day! Just from cigarettes!

Just take the State of New Jersey. They recently raised the state tax on cigarettes to $1.50 per pack. This alone raises over $200 million dollars a year for the state.

In the City of New York, besides the $1.50 per pack state tax, they also have a $1.50 per pack city tax.

Big bucks here folks. They figure, if you don't like it, you can quit.

But you can't. You're addicted.

Nice guys huh?

In Canada, the Federal government gets over two billion dollars a year from smokers. That's over five and a half million a day! We are taxed much heavier in Canada. So, in a very weird sense, a Canadian is doing a very patriotic thing by smoking. I just wish they did something useful with the money. Our country has one tenth of the population of the US and we are taxed at over three times the rate.

The Canadian government gets 21 cents per day per Canadian (including non-smokers) whereas the average American contributes only 6 cents per day. And Americans think they're patriotic. Give me a break.

4: As you can also plainly see, many people's BMWs are affected by your decision to stop smoking. Thus **the BMW dealers** won't be too thrilled either. This phenomenon is known as the trickle-down effect.

On this page do a little math.

Figure out

A: Number of years you have smoked. _____

B: Number of cigarettes per day. _____

C: Cost per pack of smokes _____

Multiply the number of cigarettes
per day (B:) by 7 and you now
know how many cigarettes
per week you smoke. _____

Multiply that number by 52
and you now know how
many cigarettes per year
you smoke. _____

Multiply that number by the cost
of a package of cigarettes and
you now know how much money
you have invested. _____

Now figure out how much money you have to earn to net that amount of money and you'll have reached a pretty startling conclusion.

Now figure out how much money a Corvette convertible costs and divide that by the amount of money you spend on cigarettes per year and you will start to see just how crazy it is to spend money on something that offers you nothing in return but bad health and an early death.

And after all of that, you still don't get the Corvette!

When you consider that the average smoker loses fifteen years of their life due to smoking, spends another fifteen years actually smoking and probably another ten to fifteen years working to earn the money to get the cigarettes in the first place, you simply cannot under any circumstance make a case for smoking.

You never see that in the ads do you?

Your Friendly Insurance Guy:

I thought Laser therapy would be a good thing for life insurance companies to offer their smoking clients free of charge. It would help their clients live longer, happier, healthier lives and stretch out the number of years they would be paying premiums.

Instead they just charge smokers higher premiums. They tell us, "Look, you smoke and we have hard, verifiable, statistical and actuarial evidence here which proves beyond a shadow of a doubt that you are going to die about seven years earlier than a non-smoker. (And by the way; the last four to five years of your life aren't going to be a real thrill either.)

With these facts in mind, we are going to have to charge you a higher premium since the likelihood of having to pay off your estate at an earlier age is so much higher. Keep in mind though that your kids will probably thank you for smoking since they will get all this insurance money a lot earlier in life due to your unfortunate early and painful death. Okay? Sign here."

What do we do? Do we do the smart thing and say, "The hell with that," and quit smoking?

No! We keep smoking! Sign there and pay the extra premiums! Only a real card-carrying, hall-of-fame schmuck would do something like that.

How do I know that?

I know because I did it.

I just quit before I got the Schmuck's 'Lifetime Achievement Award.' Lung cancer.

Those people who purchase Freedom Fifty Five insurance and smoke, aren't going to collect enough money to justify what they spent on premiums and the insurance companies know that.

Government Math:

The Canadian government would never make the treatment tax-deductible. Despite what they say, they don't really want you to quit. They desperately need the revenue for people like our beloved Mr. Chretien to give his buddies to blow on stupid golf course deals and his hundred million dollar personal jet fleet.

The government will say they want people to quit and that they raise taxes to try and get people to quit. But since over 45,000 Canadians die every year from smoking-related causes we must ask ourselves this question;

If 45,000 Canadians were dying every year in plane crashes (that's a hundred and fifty 747's every year! Just in Canada!) do you think that all the government would do is raise the taxes on plane tickets in order to get people to stop flying?

Now, let's do the same exercise in the U.S. where 430,000 people die every year from smoking related causes. That's over a thousand 747 crashes! 150,000 of the 430,000 will die from lung cancer. When you see how much money the government is willing to spend to try and nail osama bin Laden and Saddam Hussein, wouldn't you think it might be more prudent to stop the needless slaughter of American citizens by their very own corporations?

What if 215,000 US soldiers were killed in Afghanistan trying to get osama Bin Laden and then another 215,000 people had been killed in Iraq trying to get Hussein?

That's 430,000 Americans killed in just one year! Think a little shit might hit the fan over that?

But that's the number of American citizens the government allows the tobacco industry to slaughter. Not much shit hitting the fan though.

(Now I think the money spent trying to get rid of Bin Laden and Hussein and all the rest of the dorks out there who torture and kill their own citizens is money well spent. I just use the argument to try and put it all into perspective.)

Here's what Big Brother knows and isn't telling you:

1: For every thousand smokers, five hundred of you will die from smoking-related causes unless you quit.

2: 250 of you will not make it to age 65.

3: Less than nine of the thousand will die in traffic accidents. They're the lucky ones. (Probably half of them killed by drunk drivers.)

Government Intelligence? Smoking kills more people than drunk drivers but you can get into a lot more legal trouble from drinking than smoking. It's the health problems that will get the smokers. Yet the government does not act.

Very much. **They talk the talk,** (usually on CNN and their like to voters around election time) **but they don't walk the walk.**

If the government really wanted to stop smoking they would make it a lot tougher for the tobacco companies to *sell* cigarettes and *impossible* to make a profit.

One good way to put a crimp in their profits is to not let them write off any advertising and marketing expenses. They should pay taxes on revenues and then take the marketing money out of net after-tax profits. It would make the stock less attractive and force the corporate people to look for other more profitable areas to invest their money.

But our governments are too well paid by these guys and so sadly, that will not happen. They'll throw us a few bones at election time to make it look like they give a shit but do you really think they do?

If you do, read on.

A classic example of pure, unadulterated government bull-guana!

The Canadian government (Health Canada) announced on Jan 26, 2002 that over the next 5 years they are going to spend 530 million dollars to "reduce smoking in Canada." (The Globe and Mail should be happy about that. They got a full page ad out of the deal to announce the plan.)

Here's what seems a little bit weird to me about this deal. The governments (federal and provincial) take in over twenty million dollars a day in taxes thanks to smokers. That's over seven frigging billion dollars a year! Thirty six and a half billion dollars income in the next five years! And they are going to allocate 1.45% of that in their efforts to protect the citizens and "reduce smoking in Canada."

When you tax an addiction, you can raise the price to whatever you want. The true addicts will not let high prices stand between them and their 'fix.'

The only way to eliminate the problem is to eliminate the profit motive. If they can't make a buck at it, they won't do it. It's some sort of weird business thing they've been teaching at Harvard for the last two hundred years or so.

In 1999, the five largest cigarette companies in the USA spent $8.24 billion on advertising and promotion. That's over $22 million a day and $943,223 an hour. The largest category of those 'expenses' was promotional allowances which include payments to retailers for shelf space. Other expenditures are hats, lighters and multiple pack promotions.

5 Largest U.S. Cigarette Companies	
Ad $ spent in USA in 2001	$8,240,000,000.00
Per month	$686,666,666.67
Per week	$158,461,538.46
Per day	$22,575,342.47
Per hour	$943,223.00

Do you honestly believe that the government health agencies have the marketing savvy (or the desire) to try and outdo the tobacco industry? The government spends a dollar trying to get people off the weed and the tobacco company spends ten trying to convince you that it's cool.

Don't you think that $8.24 billion might be better spent trying to cure all the diseases caused by smoking? Shouldn't we be putting pressure on our politicians to do that?

Another awful reality is this; our government knows that if you smoke, you will die earlier than the people who don't smoke. This means that the non-smokers will be a burden on the (oxymoron alert) health care system and the old age pension system for an extra seven years. So in the back rooms where all the deals are made, your government believes that basically:

**"Cigarette smokers are good for the economy.
They support it with a lot of taxes
and they die earlier."**

Secondly, the tobacco lobbyists spend a lot of money to purchase the goodwill of our elected officials who make more by pandering to the interests of the nicotine delivery industry than those of the people they claim to represent.

The manufacturer gets $1.66 per pack. The wholesaler and the retailer split $.75 cents. Hardly seems worth it until you do the math and see the national number: $1,575,000,000 in

Canada. (Multiply that by ten in the U.S.A.) We don't have numbers that big in Canada.

Definitely a nice little business. Just ask Seven Eleven.

Total cost so far is $2.41 (1.66 + .75)

Now the Feds get their cut. $2.11 per pack which is a paltry twelve million a day! Total cost so far is $4.52

The Provincial governments get the rest. Consider the fact that in Ontario, a pack of smokes costs $6.75 thus giving the Ontario government a mere $2.23. In Quebec a pack of smokes costs $5.70 so they only get $1.08. In Alberta and Saskatchewan the price is $9.00 a pack so they get $4.48 per pack.

Ontario and Quebec have 62.15% of Canada's total population yet they have the lowest provincial tax rates. The cigarette companies have the most to gain by keeping the tax rate at it's lowest in those two provinces since their take in those two provinces alone, is over two billion.

Do you think the cigarette companies really give a rat's ass what goes on in Alberta and Saskatchewan? They have only 13.14% of the total market between them and their take is a lousy half billion. That's only 21% of the take in Ontario and Quebec and those big markets must be protected at all costs.

Where do you think the cigarette companies spend the bulk of their marketing/lobbying money? At least 62.05% of it. (Just vote this way Mr. MP and this little suitcase of cash is yours. Here's the keys to the condo in the Bahamas too and your airplane tickets are in the glove compartment of the limo.)

If that's not true then, why doesn't the government put the cigarette companies right out of business? It would seem to be in the best interests of the citizens. Wouldn't it? But I'm willing to bet you that will never happen.

"Smoking is the leading cause of statistics."

Now let's take the USA. As I mentioned earlier, the Federal government takes in six billion dollars annually in taxes from smoking. Yet, the US taxpayers pay $38 billion a year in federal taxes to treat the many health problems caused by smoking. (Don't forget that the government lets them spend $8.24 billion to promote that habit.)

Let me see now, you take in 6 and you spend 38. That sounds like something only a government would do.

Or could do. And they're doing it with our money!

But leaving that point aside, do you think that smokers should pay the thirty two billion in taxes to cover the shortfall? Or should the non-smokers continue helping to pay that bill?

According to data gleaned form the *American Lung Association* website, the *Centers For Disease Control And Prevention* estimates that **each pack of cigarettes sold in the United States *costs* the country $7.18 in medical care costs and lost productivity!**

This breaks down to $3.45 per pack in health care costs and $3.73 in job productivity lost because of premature death from smoking.

Why are we making the non-smokers pay for the health problems of the smokers? Wouldn't it make sense to have an extra $7.18 tax added to each pack of cigarettes to compensate for that?

Think about this: "Why are we letting the tobacco companies take profits when we are charging non-smokers for the problems that those profits have caused?"

Even now, the tobacco industry has been ordered to pay $246 billion dollars in tobacco-related health care costs to the 50 US states. But most states have failed to spend the money as it was intended; to fund tobacco prevention and control programs. This despite the fact that states with laws that encourage people to stop have fewer smokers. The governments know that it works but they just don't do it. Why?

Who knows for sure but if I could hazard a guess it would be that they know that they won't be held accountable for it and they can just go ahead and do whatever the hell they want and nobody's going to gripe about it because they won't even basically know.

This needs to be looked at, yet sadly I doubt that will ever happen. Why? Because somebody in government will stop it from happening. Why? Because they will benefit financially by doing so.

Will they ever admit it? It is the ultimate act of naivete to believe that they would. Heads will roll in order to stop that from happening. There is simply too much money involved.

Did you know: That 75% of senators in the U.S.A., Republican and Democrat, take money from tobacco companies? Now, do you think the tobacco company would support a senator with a campaign contribution if they knew he was voting against their best interests and voting in the actual interests of the people who elected them?

From 1990 to 2004 the tobacco industry 'donated' $51,550,456 to political parties in the USA to help get various people elected. It is also interesting to note that 75.02% of that money, ($38,672,511) went to the Republican party and 24.98% of that money ($12,877,955) went to the Democrats.

Jackie Mason said it best: *"It is more profitable for your Congressman to support the tobacco industry than your life."*

Blood money?

Caroline Waxler, A New York based financial writer has published a book called: *Stocking up on Sin: How to Crush the Market with Vice-based Investing.* In this book she advises readers to exploit their moral depravity for financial gain. In other words, to profit from people's nasty habits instead of moralizing about them. Her sample "sindex" includes 69 stocks that represent vice, avarice and social irresponsibility. Sex, booze, drugs, gambling and tobacco are all in there. So is war or as they like to call it, ' The Defence Sector.'

She agrees that there's no argument that what tobacco companies produce is addictive and harmful and can be fatal. That's more than the tobacco industry will admit to, but nobody is forcing anyone to smoke. I might argue that point. I think they are preying on people, lying and in a cold-blooded fashion taking advantage of people's basically trusting nature.

She goes on to say that while lawsuits against the tobacco industry abound, the landscape is much different overseas. She notes that tobacco investments are worth considering because they have what every product should have: customer loyalty and a recurring stream of revenue.

Can you imagine that? Being loyal to as well as giving your money on a daily basis to somebody who is making something that will kill you. Now I ask you; Is that the act of a sane person?

Stop giving them your money for cigarettes and buy their stock instead. Your dividend cheques will be blood money but as they like to say, "Money is money."

And if you're lucky, you just might live long enough to spend it.

Stage 2: Get Mad. Get Mad As Hell!

Aldous Huxley wrote, "Ye shall know the truth and the truth shall make you mad."

- **Get mad at the cigarette companies** for outright lying to us and manipulating us.

- **Get mad at the government** for letting the cigarette companies lie to us.

- **Get mad at yourself:**
  - For naively believing all the bullshit and wasting all that money over the years.
  - For not having the inner strength to make up your own mind.
  - For not checking the facts out for yourself. I mean really, what the hell did John Wayne really know how to do except how to act. Wait a minute. He didn't even know how to do that! He said he reacted.

Fred Flinstone was once a spokesman for a cigarette company. Do you believe it?

Fred 'Frigging' Flinstone!

I discovered that the cigarette companies stated "for the record" under oath, to a federal commission, that they **"never have marketed and never will market"** their products to kids. It was later revealed that they were in fact, marketing to a sector of society, which they categorized as **"non-adults."**

Non-adults! Do you believe that bull****?

Are you mad yet? Read on.

In 1994 a bunch of tobacco company execs stated under oath and to the man that, "I believe that cigarette smoking is not addictive." To me, that's like believing the Enron Executive who got a five million dollar stock option bonus for running the company and then states to the Congress that he had, "no idea any of that other shit was going on." He just knew about the legal stuff.

Think about the perjury angle and ask yourself why nobody ever goes down for that. It makes me believe that **CEOs are really just people who, for a ridiculous amount of money, will portray themselves as the absolute dumbest assholes on the planet.**

If you were a 7-Eleven manager and you gave that excuse to your boss; that you didn't know any of that illegal stuff was going on, you would be shot and it would be considered justifiable homicide at the Harvard School Of Business.

Yet, a lot of the dorks who use that cop-out graduated from Harvard.

Think about 'Joe Camel.'

He's cool. He's also very dangerous.

B-J (Before Joe Nyuk Nyuk), Camels were smoked by 1% of US smokers under the age of 18. Now thanks to the cool 'Joe Camel' promotion, they get a third of that market and the five hundred million in sales that goes with it. And.. smoking in that age group has increased 10% since that campaign started. When I learned that 90% of all smokers started before they turned 21 and 60% started before they turned 14, I could understand their marketing strategy; *'get them addicted when they're young'* and you've got a hundred thousand dollar addict in your customer data base.

I'm at Desperado's bar in Calgary at the Calgary Stampede in 2001. Just over one year off the weed. About four thousand people are in there drinking, dancing, listening to music and basically just trying to get lucky. Generally having a hell of a good time.

This outstandingly good-looking young woman all dressed in a skimpy black and gold lame mini skirt, cowboy hat and sexy black 'shitkicker' boots, came strolling in. She set up a little gold booth and started handing out Benson & Hedges cigarettes. Free of charge. To anybody that wanted one. Her pitch; "Come on. Try it. You'll like it."

The idea here is to get them partying, get them a little pissed, give them some free smokes and then get them hooked.

The result: They get a customer and the customer gets a death sentence.

I walked over to her and she smiled and offered me a package of smokes. I asked her, "Does your daddy know what you do for a living?"

She told me, "My daddy works for the company." He not only knew what she was doing, he knew what he was doing.

Young people go to 'parties' at nightclubs with professional DJs. Guess who pays to bring them in? And they say they aren't marketing to our kids.

Papa was a Rolling Stone but I'll never be one.

The Camel people even ran the Joe Camel promo in Rolling Stone Magazine which is why you will never read this story in that magazine. (To do so is called 'pissing in the soup') Those hip, leading edge, anti-establishment, cool, in-your-face-with-the-truth people are really just a bunch of ruthless, unprincipled, money-hungry, yuppie-slime sons of bitches.

Knowing that the demographics of their readership is conducive to the target market of the cigarette companies, they ran the ads, took the money and in so doing, they revealed themselves for what they really are. (Even though I love the magazine they will never again get one dime of my money.)

We make it tougher for the tobacco companies to market their products in North America so they develop newer, more sophisticated marketing tactics for North America and using the old tactics, they develop new markets in other countries.

The US government even lobbies on behalf of the US tobacco companies to have foreign governments allow the cigarette companies to advertise and market their products in the very ways that are banned by that government in the USA.

Talk about two-faced. They probably figure it's a good method of population control.

It's like the Catholic Church. They forbid the pill but they let you smoke. That must be their form of birth control. Have more babies but don't let them live as long.

Maybe they just got a better offer from the tobacco companies than the pharmaceutical industry.

Terminator meets *Fast And Furious:*

One of the more sophisticated marketing tactics that they use to promote smoking is the movies. The more times an adolescent sees movie characters smoke, the more receptive that child is to the idea of taking up smoking, according to Dartmouth College researchers.

In the April 2002 issue of the *American Journal of Preventive Medicine* lead author James D. Sargent, a doctor at Dartmouth Medical School states, "Movies are a powerful socializing force for contemporary adolescents, shaping views of what is 'cool,' attractive and grown-up. (I wonder if the folks who made "Casablanca" knew that) With increasing restrictions on public tobacco use, movies have become a key way that adolescents learn about the social context of tobacco use."

The researchers indexed the amount of smoking in 600 movies and allowed students to choose 50 movies to watch. They correlated the amount of smoking in the movies and measured the child's vulnerability to starting smoking.

The results reveal a strong relationship between viewing tobacco use in movies and more positive attitudes toward smoking among adolescent never-smokers, Sargent reports. Seeing a lot of smoking in movies also led to lower resistance to their peers' offers to smoke, and a stronger belief that smoking is a normal adult behavior.

The more times an adolescent sees movie characters smoke, the more receptive that child is to the idea of taking up smoking, according to the Dartmouth College researchers. I imagine they want the 'cool' people to be perceived as smokers.

Mixed messages? I'd say so. Check out Bruce Willis, Jean Claude Van Damme, Kurt Russel, Val Kilmer, Brad Pitt, Sharon Stone, Samuel L. Jackson, John Travolta, Robert De Niro, Nicolas Cage, William Hurt and Kathleen Turner, in all those 'cool' movies; Die Hard, Tombstone, Body Heat, Basic Instinct, Fast and Furious, Jackie Brown, Pulp Fiction, The Long Kiss Goodnight, Raging Bull, Casino and hundreds more

Stanton Glantz, a professor of medicine at the University of California, San Francisco, in a study funded by the National Cancer Institute, found that on average, in 2000, the 20 top grossing films featured 50% more instances of smoking per hour than in 1960. An American Lung Association survey discovered that 61% of the tobacco use in films in 2001 occurred in movies rated G, PG, and PG-13.

Want to see smoking? Watch *Charlie's Angels*. Or *Save The Last Dance* or *In The Bedroom*. They got Hackadamey Awards from The American Lung Association.

Rob Reiner, (*Meathead*) and president of Castle Rock Entertainment says, "Movies are basically advertising cigarettes to kids. If your movie has the "F" word twice, you get rated "R." Imagine that! Our kids can watch them smoke but they can only hear the "F" word twice. That's bull doo doo folks. Pure bull doo doo. (Now the kids can read this.)

Parents see more smoking in movies and TV and they figure, "What the hell? The kids'll never believe me, I'm not as cool as those people." Their resistance to the idea is lowered and more kids take up smoking and get less heat from their parents. The government will give you all sorts of statistics saying that fewer young people are smoking but even the young people don't believe that.

Believe me folks. These people are bastards. And they only do it for one reason. Greed. You give them your money to ruin your life and they try to make you feel that it's essentially a 'cool' thing for you to do. Why?

Because way down deep they think you're a schmuck.

"The tobacco companies *must* get their customers to adopt the habit at a young age or they will never get them."

Some information found at the Fred Hutchison Cancer Research Center says:

"Statistics show that if a child reaches 18 without becoming a smoker, his or her odds of remaining smoke-free are around 90 percent."

They have to get them when they're young.

Just like they got me. And I'll lay you ten to one that's when they got you.

Their business model depends on getting young people to smoke. Do you know anybody over the age of thirty who had never smoked and then started smoking?

I only know one guy who started smoking when he was forty and he was in jail. Cancer was the least of his problems.

I think by the age of 30, everybody pretty much realizes that it's about the worst thing you can do. They know that to start smoking would be a ridiculous decision. By that age you are usually fairly well informed about life and financial issues.

You know by then that to start smoking now, would be very bad for your health and a stupid financial decision. People over thirty who have never smoked will look at smokers and ask, "Why do you do that? Don't you know that it's not only bad for your health but it's like a total waste of a lot of money?"

I read statistical data all the time which says that fewer young people are smoking than ever before. Thus the government sponsored associations that offer programs to help people quit smoking, can justify their existence, economically.

In December of 2000, the Fred Hutchison Cancer Research Institute in Seattle published an article in *the Journal of the National Cancer Institute* and found, based on a 15-year study, that **programs teaching youth how to identify and resist social influences to smoke, the main focus of smoking-prevention education and research for more than two decades, simply do not work.**

They needed to do that in order to provide 'hard' data that said it didn't work. So they couldn't get sued by the tobacco companies for slander and other scurrilous comments. It's like watching the weather channel to find out how the weather is instead of looking out the window.

Think about it. On one hand we have the sophisticated marketing techniques aimed at our kids urging them to smoke and eat at MacDonald's, and on the other hand, the bureaucratic efforts of some agencies whose heart is in the right place but really have their hands tied in the good fight.

They can't win. **It's really up to us.**

If I waited for Stats Can or the US statistics people to publish their data I would be making travel decisions long after the train had left the station.

I like to go to the 'street.' Talk to young people who smoke and ask them things like:

A: "Why do you smoke?

B: "Do you think there are more or less young people who smoke today?"

The answer to the first question is usually, **"because it's cool."** I am not amazed by that. That's why I started. Way back on page 17.

The answer to the second question is always, **"Most of my friends smoke.** I'd say that most of the young people my age smoke." The tobacco industry calls it the 'old peer pressure trick.'

I'm telling you that I do not believe the data I hear from the *'system.'* I do believe what I see with my own two eyes. When I see a lot of young people smoking and telling me that most of their friends smoke, and then I turn around and hear the government and other bureaucratic institutions telling us that fewer young people are smoking today, I ask myself why the things I see with my own two eyes do not gibe with the things they tell me.

I believe that **the 'system' wants you to think that smoking is on the decrease.** They don't really want to alarm you by telling you that their efforts are not really working. That would be bad for business (and job security.) They fear that you would want to make them accountable for their actions and they would not get their funding.

Thus they present us with endless streams of data which show that their efforts are bearing fruit. But, the Fred Hutchison Cancer research Institute in December, 2000 stated their findings from a 15 year long study on the effects of anti smoking programs on youth: *"Surprisingly and disappointingly, we found a striking similarity in smoking prevalence between the experimental and control groups,"* says Dr. Art Peterson, *a professor of biostatistics at the University of Washington.* ***"It's disappointing because we know that youth need our help to withstand the considerable forces that are out there. The*** *social pressures, whether from tobacco advertising, marketing or peer pressure. They need our help, and we were not able to identify a program that succeeded."*

Now ask yourself this. If the Fred Hutchison Institution people took 15 years to do an independent study which came to that conclusion, do you think that maybe the authorities who operate these programs already knew that answer beforehand? If so why didn't they tell us that their programs were virtually ineffective?

Because we would have raised hell and their funding would have been pulled back. We would have looked for other ways. We might even have taken on the responsibility for keeping our kids from smoking ourselves. (One idea I liked is to not shop in a store that displays cigarettes for sale in front of our kids. Especially a store that accepts payments from cigarette companies for shelf space.)

The tobacco industry spends billions marketing their product. The governments get billions in taxes. The governments spend a pittance on prevention practices to satisfy the 'tree huggers.'

They will tell you that smoking is on the decline in order to reduce the pressure we put on them. "Hey, we're doing something about it. See? According to our numbers, smoking is down."

There is an old courtroom saying that "figures can lie and liars can figure." I'm sure you've heard that before.

Do you believe what you see or what *they* tell you? If you believe what *they* tell you, then you should give yourself a rectal examination because I think your head is already in the ideal position to do it.

Low tar? Light cigarettes?
Safe Smoking?
My ass!

And it will be your ass too if you believe all that bull. If you really are naïve enough to think that *"light"* cigarettes will reduce your smoking risk, just ask Sarah Brady, wife of Reagan White House Press Secretary, James Brady.

She is 'dying from lung cancer,' caused, she says, by smoking Marlboro *lights*. To prove how addictive smoking is, she has been fighting lung cancer for the last year and she still can't kick the habit! But I don't think that's the whole story. If a doctor told you that you had terminal lung cancer would you quit? What's the point? Keep on smoking. It's all over anyway. (But it would bother me to keep giving even more money to the very people who were killing me.)

What happens when you smoke *'light'* cigarettes is that you **smoke more** or **smoke *harder*** in order to get your *fix*. You just mix more air with the smoke but your system is till looking for its *'hit.'* **You need a certain amount of nicotine to get the hit and whether you mix it with air or not, that's what you are going to go for.**

I remember trying the really light cigarettes and how my head nearly caved in from trying to suck in the amount of smoke I needed to get off on my endorphin hit. What they know is this, "they keep on sucking until they get the endorphin hit." One drag on the heavy duty ones and five drags on the "Ultra-Light" ones. It's the hit we're going for. They know that.

The R.J. Reynolds Tobacco Company, in a 1982 interoffice memorandum stated that, *"Such cigarettes, while deceptive in the extreme, would be very difficult for the consumer to resist, since they would provide everything that we presently believe makes for desirable products: taste, 'punch,' ease of draw and 'low FTC tar.'"*

They have admitted here that they know people are aware that smoking is unhealthy and they are looking for some reason, *any reason*, that can help them justify their actions. "Well, at least what I'm doing is not as harmful as the guy who smokes plain *Camels*. They have no filters and they're not light. Those guys will die a lot sooner than me."

They probably never stopped to notice that the Camel smoker doesn't need to take as many drags to get where he needs to be. Smoking plain, unfiltered heavy duty *Camels* just gets you there sooner.

People who smoke 'light' cigarettes probably believe that ordering a diet coke will magically turn their *Whoppers* and *french fries* into health food.

You can believe whatever you want to believe but the cold hard facts are that this smoking addiction/ habit will kill you. And your children.

A note about the anger thing.

Some people have told me that it's not 'healthy' to be angry. I should not in good conscience recommend it.

I ask them, "So you're saying don't get angry. Smoke cigarettes instead. That's better than being angry?"

They say, "No. Of course not. I just don't think it's good to recommend any more anger in the world."

I say, "It's tough to suck and blow at the same time. **I recommend the anger thing mainly because it worked for me and people can do a lot when they're angry. Besides, fifteen years of being angry beats fifteen years of being dead. It beats the hell out of it. I know because I'm living those fifteen years right now. Sure, I'm angry but at least I ain't dead."**

CHAPTER 12

Stage 3: Be Afraid. Be Very Afraid.

When I began my career in sales I was told that people act out of two reasons and only two reasons. *Fear* of loss and *desire* to gain.

This is what you should be afraid of:

- Afraid of **dying too young.**
- Afraid of the **pain** that comes with lung cancer and the other diseases.
- Afraid of a **drastic reduction in the quality** of the last years of your life.

A WHO (World Health Organization) report indicates that tobacco **"causes more deaths than all other forms of substance abuse combined."** It kills three million people a year worldwide. That's one every ten seconds!

One American every minute.

One Canadian every ten minutes. (We do have the advantage of a relatively small population.)

According to the Statistics Canada and the Canadian Cancer Society, lung cancer is the leading cause of death for both men and women in Canada; In 2003, 10,900 men and 7,900 women for a total of 19,800 Canadians, died from lung cancer.

I nearly lost my mind when I learned that we are working on our 3rd 'Marlboro Man.' The first two actually died of lung cancer. I saw the 1st actual Marlboro Man himself in a TV program on *A&E*. Sitting there on his horse, looking very small and frail. Staring at what was surely one of his last sunsets. But he wasn't smoking anymore.

Too late big fella.

Walt Disney died of lung cancer at age 65 and his son in law, Bob Brown, died of lung cancer at age 38. Walt Disney, probably one of the smartest and most creative people of the 20th century.

He literally had it all. He owned Disneyland! He hung out with the real Mickey Mouse! But he smoked and he died not only a stupid and painful death, he died an early one.

His daughter's husband obviously didn't learn anything from that. So fear itself will often not be enough to motivate you to quit.

In Canada, they now put pictures of cancer-infested lungs and tar-clogged heart valves on the covers of the packages to help discourage smokers. I'm glad I quit before they did that. I would have felt even stupider paying all that money to buy a product which graphically depicted all the horrible things it could do to me.

It brings to mind Bill Hick's classic bit on smoking.

Two guys are buying cigarettes at the party store. One guy looks at the picture on his package and asks the other guy, 'What kind are you smoking?'

'Throat polyps. What are you smoking?'

'Low birth weight. I can live with that. I just don't buy the ones that say cancer.'

Out of the woods?

The Fred Hutchison Cancer Research Center published an article in the July, 2003 issue of Cancer Epidemiology, Biomarkers and Prevention. It stated that; "long-term, heavy smoking doubles that risk of more aggressive prostate cancer in middle-aged men. Specifically, men under 65 with a history of 40 or more 'pack-years' (those who smoke a pack a day for 40 years or two packs a day for 20 years) of cigarette smoking face a 100% increased risk, – or double the risk – of developing more aggressive forms of the disease as compared to nonsmokers."

The risk returns to normal in ten years. That's ten years after you quit. That's a little fear bonus that I will carry around inside me until 2010.

I'd like to thank the tobacco industry and the government for that little bit of stress. Thanks boys.

Now find a way to turn the stress into anger and use it to send you over the top in your quest to quit. Don't hold it in. That's bad for you. When you meet somebody from the tobacco industry tell them that they are murderous, devious people. They are the scum of the earth. They can't even sue you for libel or defamation of character because it's all true. So, "lay on Macduff. And damn'd be him that first cries, "Hold, enough."

Know ye this:

- There are certain doors in life that we have to walk through alone. Death is one of them. If you've ever watched someone die, you will realize that they are going through that door all alone. You can empathize and you can sympathize but you cannot do it for them. And you can't change the result.
- **The cigarette companies will not feel the least bit of your pain nor will they go through that door with you. They will only send you through it fifteen years sooner and in a lot more pain as well as making you pay a lot of money for the privilege. If they feel any regret at all it's only because they lost a customer.**

In June of 2001, Richard Boeken, was awarded $3,000,000,000 in damages by a jury after he sued Philip Morris. (Note: that's billion.)

The basis for his suit was that the tobacco company had portrayed smoking as a cool thing to do and concealed its dangers from him.

A Superior court judge later reduced that amount to a paltry $100 million dollars. A spokesman for the tobacco company stated that, "We still believe the verdict was incorrect and will continue to pursue the appeal."

The guy said it with a straight face too.

He should. He's a lawyer.

The tobacco company's legal team has kept the appeal in court and Mr. Boeken died of lung cancer at the age of 57, in January of 2002. (He smoked two packs of Marlboros a day for 40 years.) His estate will get any of the money if the case ever gets out of the courts.

Whaddya wanna bet that's ever gonna happen?

Not.

In October, 2002 a California jury ordered Philip Morris to pay 28 billion dollars in damages to a 64 year old woman with lung cancer. She claimed that she had smoked since she was seventeen and that **the company had deceived her into thinking that smoking was safe. The tobacco company deliberately concealed what it knew about the link between smoking and lung cancer.**

If Philip Morris ever paid her that amount, she would be immediately vaulted to the number three position on Forbes' World's richest list behind Bill Gates and Warren Buffet, (by the way neither of these guys smoke and both are thought by many to be pretty smart guys.)

Now the company says that she should have been more aware of the health risks associated with smoking which basically means that they knew all along that it was dangerous.

Did you get that? The tobacco company, which has sworn under oath that they thought it was good for you, has now admitted that they know it's not good for you.

Mixed message?

The sad truth is that the tobacco companies make more money by hiring lawyers to keep the issue in court than they do by paying off. I think that if anybody ever really gets paid, the precedent will bring such a flood of lawsuits that the entire industry will find itself sued out of existence. Thus the courts will be tied up in these decisions for years.

The courts are where *justice* goes to die.

CHAPTER 13

Stage # 4: *Now* Call 911... and get some help.

Laser therapy, is it virtual reality or real virtuality? I don't really know for sure. I think it depends on who you ask. I would never ask a doctor or a pharmacist. The doctor would probably try to schedule me for surgery. The pharmacist would probably tell me it's all in my mind. A *'drugs are the true path to salvation'* kind of thing.

The medical and pharmaceutical industry PR spin-doctors will probably say that laser therapy is all witch doctor stuff. It must be. **It's relatively inexpensive, very effective and totally outside of their control.**

A smart man once told me, "If you think you can or you can't, you're probably right." The laser people will simply tell you that it works. But only if you really want it to work.

It worked for me.

I do want to mention here that I am not trying to tell you that laser therapy is the only way to go. I personally think it's a great way but that's mainly because for me, it worked. But I'm sure the other methods would have worked too.

That's why I said, "Call 911." The patch, the pill, hypnosis, audio tapes, acupuncture and any other smoking cessation program will all help you stop once you bring these three other elements to the table with you.

Logic: – you need to know deep inside your brain that it's not a smart thing to do. There is absolutely no financial justification for doing it. It's like this total rip-off dude.

Fear: – You need to be really afraid of what will happen if you start or if you fail to stop. It's going to be horrible. Everyone, to a man or woman, who is going through it will tell you that. Nobody who has gone through it can tell you that because they are dead.

Anger: – Definitely the strongest motivation of them all for me. I am furious at the tobacco industry, the various governments and their lying, two-faced politicians. And ultimately, **I'm angry at myself for being so quick to let the media and the rest of the system do my thinking for me.**

When the temptation to light up was at its strongest, it was my **anger that got me through it.** I would not give one more dime to those horrible, rotten, lousy, lying, deceitful, despicable people.

Once you have gone through this process and learned for yourself, firsthand what this is all about, you begin to experience a feeling welling up inside you. Your pride will want you to stop spending your hard earned money. Money which you spend hours, days, weeks and months of every year to earn just so you can give it to those merchants of evil who will ultimately reward you with a horrible death. Once you begin to see what you are doing in that light, you will begin to get the feeling.

You will know that you must quit. You have to quit. There is no way you can not quit. You want to quit more than anything.

You want to be free.

FREE AT LAST!

One More Time:

> **1: Get angry,**
> **2: Be afraid,**
> **3: Do the math,**
> **4: Get some help.**

Ann Landers told me one day: Actually I read it in her column, but if Ann Landers printed it, the numbers must be true. "A study published in the British Medical Journal, tracked the rising death toll in China where two thirds of all males become smokers. Their findings were awesome.

- China is home to 20 percent of the world's population and consumes a third of the world's cigarettes.
- The study found that 25 % of all the deaths of Chinese people in Hong Kong in 1998, ages 35 to 69, were attributable to tobacco.
- There are 300 million smokers in China – more than the entire US population.
- They consume 1.7 *trillion* cigarettes per year.
- That's 3 million cigarettes per minute!

If those numbers don't make you want to kick the habit, what will it take?"

Is this the path for you?

Smokers who've known me as a long time nicotine addict often ask me, "How the hell did you do it?"

I tell them this same story you are reading now. Then I give them the phone number. (1 800 807 8714) Some of them have gone. Now they don't smoke either. Some procrastinate. Just as I did. And that is why I wrote this story down.

Ike Turner once said in an interview, when asked about his battles with drugs, that **he never met anybody on drugs, who didn't want to get off them.** I think that's true of most of the smokers I've known.

I have heard the odd smoker say that they enjoyed it too much to quit. I wouldn't trade places with them if they had Warren Buffet's money, Hugh Hefner's girlfriends and could play the guitar like Eric Clapton.

I saw *rock'n roll* legend **Ronnie Hawkins** in a TV interview. The man is well over sixty years old and he looks like he's been rode hard and put up wet more than a few times. I bought his first album in 1955 and I've been watching him play in bars ever since.

He talked about his battles with drugs and alcohol. How he had done them all and had been able to quit them all... except for cigarettes.

"They are the toughest drug of them all to quit."

He went on to say that he quit once and; **"it was the roughest half hour of my life."**

A Voyage to the *Dark Side*

I attended a class at Eastern Michigan University in the Criminology department doing some research for a novel I was writing. The guest lecturer was an Investigative Sergeant for the Ypsilanti police department. His guests were two recovering crack-cocaine addicts who had supported their 15 year drug habits as prostitutes.

They had been off the stuff and off the streets for five months. I really felt for them as I got a sense of the hell that their lives had become.

During a question period, I asked the girls if either one of them had ever smoked cigarettes. One of the girls had never smoked cigarettes. The other girl had smoked since her teen age years.

She still smoked.

Could not quit!

She gave up a fifteen year crack-cocaine habit but could not quit cigarettes! **If you smoke and cannot quit, do not come down too hard on crack addicts. They have a better quit rate than you do.**

The sergeant added that he too smoked and could not give it up. Yet, **crack-cocaine is not legal and cigarette smoking is.**

The message? **Make up your own mind.** Think for yourself. Know that **most of what you read is advertising. Motivational material designed to compel you to give your money to people who do not have your best interests in mind.**

A sad, sad story:

One of Canada's all time favourite Canadians: Peter Gzowski, wrote an article, published in The Globe And Mail on Sept. 8, 2001. It was about his 50 year, 75 cigarette a day addiction.

Title: "Out Of Breath."

Let's do the math first. A 75 cigarette a-day habit is 2,281 a month. That's 27,375 cigarettes per year for a 50 year total of 1,368,750! He spent over $250,000 on his addiction! After tax dollars too. His picture probably hangs in the tobacco companies' 'Hall of Fame.'

He told how he had tried all the conventional ways of quitting many times over the years and not been able to kick. He finally went to a private clinic and ultimately stopped smoking. It was 1999 when he did it.

It was too late. Ironically, *after* he quit he developed emphysema. When he wrote the article he had a 'hose in his nose." The doctors call it **COPD, for *Chronic Obstructive Pulmonary Disease.*** It's a nice little combination of emphysema and chronic bronchitis and **15 to 20 per cent of you smokers will get it.**

He died in January 2002. He was a hell of a guy but he made one huge mistake. He smoked and he waited too long to quit. Now he's dead. Smoking killed him. **He gave the tobacco companies a quarter of a million dollars and then they killed him.** They got him hooked when he was a kid and he followed the path of addiction that they knew from the outset he would. And that is just what they'll do to you.

Peter died at age 67. As he so eloquently put it: *"If you've decided to quit you will: if you haven't you should get your affairs in order."*

The Aftermath

CHAPTER 14

Everybody Must Get Stoned?
Or,
"Endorhpins, that's what it's really all about but, do we have to smoke to get them?"

Think about it now, if somebody came up to you and said, "Would you like an endorphin hit?" What are you going to do? "Just say no."

Probably not.

Let's face it. Endorphin hits feel good.

Real good.

It's not your body that feels it either. It's your brain.

Because your brain decides what feels good. You kiss an ugly girl or a pretty girl. The physical sensation is the same. The brain decides whether or not you like what's going on and whether or not to try and go to the next level.

Intoxication of some type has been a quest for mankind ever since the dawn of time. And probably for several years before that. When someone asks you, "Would you like an endorphin hit?" what they are really asking you is, "Would you like to feel better than you do right now?"

Of course you would, unless you are some kind of weird mystical guru that sleeps on a bed of nails, in which case all he has to do to feel better is get out of bed.

Who in their right mind would say no to an orgasm? "No thanks. I think I'll pass." Reminds me of the guy in the psychiatrist's office when the shrink says;

"Describe the worst orgasm of your life."

The guy replies, "Fabulous."

You've got to understand what you are doing when you smoke. That is a key point. You are not really giving in to an addiction.

You are going after an endorphin hit. Just like Jody told me at the laser session.

Once you see that what you are really doing is looking for an endorphin hit, then what you should do is look for another way to get it. The brain will tell you when you get there. Not your lungs.

What they are:

Endorphins are neurotransmitters found in the brain that have pain-relieving properties similar to morphine. They are probably the best and most legal way to get high. They are why soldiers wounded in battle can continue to fight. They account for a phenomenon known as the runner's high. They are why some people are drawn to dangerous activities like car racing, sky diving and bungee jumping.

The 3 major types of endorphins and where they can be found:

Beta endorpins, found primarily in the pituitary gland. The other two are **Enkephalin** and **Dynorphin.** Both are distributed at various points throughout the nervous system.

How they do what they do:

They are believed to produce four key effects on the body/mind: they enhance the immune system, they relieve pain, they reduce stress and they postpone the aging process.

Endorphins interact with opiate receptor neurons to reduce the intensity of pain. Among individuals afflicted with chronic pain disorders, endorphins are often found in high numbers. Many painkilling drugs, such as morphine and codeine, act like endorphins and actually activate opiate receptors.

How to have fun with them:

Besides behaving as a pain regulator, endorphins are also *thought* to be connected to physiological processes including euphoric feelings, appetite modulation, and the release of sex hormones.

Prolonged, continuous exercise contributes to an increased production and release of endorphins, resulting in a sense of euphoria that has been popularly labeled "the runner's high." They also produce what is known as the "second wind."

The release of endorphins into your system is what cigarettes are all about. **If they didn't do that, there would be no reason to smoke them.** We all want endorphins to work their special magic on us. **What we need is a new way to do it.**

According to the "Ask Alice" website at Columbia University; "Some researchers believe that strenuous exercise releases endorphins into the blood stream. **Others agree that endorphins are released during orgasm, as well as during laughter.**

Endorphins are formed within the body and they have a similar chemical structure to morphine. In addition to their analgesic affect, endorphins are thought to be involved in controlling the body's response to stress, regulating contractions of the intestinal wall, and determining mood. They may also regulate the release of hormones from the pituitary gland, notably growth hormone and the gonadotropin hormones. (If they're what I think they are, they're my faves.)

It seems that endorphin stimulation may occur with frequent sex and masturbation, yet Alice doesn't know of any evidence at the moment that too much sex (or exercise or laughter, for that matter) and consequential elevated levels of endorphins would have any kind of reverse effect – i.e. depletion of bodily endorphins, depression, etc. As we speak, there is current research being done to elucidate the full range of endorphins' functions in the body."

Alice shouldn't worry about too much sex, though...

Listen to this girls.

(guys be sure you show this part to your loved one):

In a 10-year study involving 3500 people, Dr. David Weeks, a neuropsychologist at the Royal Edinburgh Hospital and author of *Secrets of the Super Young* (Berkley, 1999) found that men and women who have sex four to five times a week look more than ten years younger than the average person, who *only* has sex twice a week. Dr. Weeks believes that the pleasure derived from sex was a crucial factor in preserving youth. "It makes us happy and produces chemicals (endorphins and oxytocin) telling us so."

Makes sense to me.

What they are saying here is that lots of sex not only produces lots of endorphins it also helps combat the advanced aging effects of your smoking habit. The message is; quit smoking and have lots of sex. You'll live longer. And die with a smile on your face which I can guarantee you will not do if you continue to smoke.

More endorphin producing stuff:

Meditation, deep breathing, ribald laughter, eating spicy food or even from receiving acupuncture treatments or chiropractic adjustments. (I did not get paid by the Chiropractic Association to say that but I can see how that would do it.)

Also eating chocolate and certain types of music. Tex-Mex, Thai food, Mexican food, Cajun food, Chinese (especially

Szechuan) and just about anything with chili peppers which provide a stimulating "bite" that increases the body's production of endorphins.

Here's what I like to do.

I read my joke book, "**The Joy Of The Joke**" every day. Laughter is like aerobics for the insides. They say that doing so will release endorphins into your system. I agree with that. Laughter makes you feel good and that's endorphins man. Like the Reader's Digest people say, "Laughter is the best medicine."

The ultimate endorphin hit.

I bought a mountain bike with the money I saved. A nice one. I ride it everywhere. After twelve to fifteen minutes flat out, I can get my own personal, hard-earned endorphin hit. I'm up to three or four a day now. I told my mother, "Don't worry, I'm just going to do it until I need glasses."

Know something?

An endorphin hit feels a lot better when you really earn it. It's sort of like seducing a beautiful woman versus paying for a cheap hooker. The same thing ultimately happens but you feel a lot better about yourself after one experience than the other.

You get back from a bike ride. You're sweating. Your heart is beating fast. You feel like a million bucks. You drink some water. Your system feels like its working. Running on all eight cylinders.

You will also *feel* the thrill of victory that comes from beating your smoking habit.

Even better.

You don't want a cigarette. Believe me. It will not even begin to make you feel as good as you feel after the ride.

We drink, we smoke, we make love, we eat Mexican food, Cajun food and Thai food, we eat chocolate, we ride our bikes.

Why?

Endorphins man. Doing it feels better than not doing it.
A lot better. At least it feels different. And if you want to feel different, *different better* beats *different worse*. By a long way.

I'm down to drinking, riding my bike and making love. (As Rodney says, "Now all I need is other people!")

Endorphin hits are not that hard to get. **You just need to know what to look for and how to do it.**

A lady once told a shrink on TV that she didn't enjoy sex. The shrink said, "Well there is only one reason why you don't."

"What's that," she asked?

"You're doing it wrong."

Surely by now you must agree that if you smoke to get an endorphin hit, you're doing it wrong?

I decided that if I'm going to get an endorphin hit, I'm going to get a good one. Not one of those *cheap, lousy, rotten, stinkin'* endorphin hits that you get from cigarettes.

That works well for me.

Plus

I'll still be getting my endorphin hits long after the smokers are dead and buried.

Dear Mr. Disney,

Y'a should have quit Walt. We all miss you. Disney World misses you. The world could really use a guy like you these days. Your work has produced and still does produce a lot of endorphins.

CHAPTER 15
Your Drug Of Choice?

Imagine that you're a corporate executive trying to make a decision on which drug you should choose to take to market. Tobacco or heroin. (By the way, if you think you might like to try heroin, which interestingly enough was invented by the Bayer Corporation, I recommend you try watching "Trainspotting.")

I think 'The Hawk" was right.

Tobacco is the hardest drug to get off.

If you want to get into the endorphin hit business, tobacco is the best long-term investment. Heroin addicts don't live that long. Alcoholics go down hill pretty fast as do pill poppers and coke-heads.

Tobacco is the most long term profitable way to go. It will still kill you, it just won't seem like it until it's too late.

Besides, there is so much money involved in the business that the companies can't quit now. **Only the marketplace can kill the tobacco business.** The government just kind of goes along for the ride. Hand in hand with big business. That's what they do.

Why?

Again with the greed thing. Tobacco industry lobbyists and their allies in Congress can get more done to enhance the opportunities for the cigarette industry than the agencies who really only have God and the best interest of the people on their side. Politics and big business are only interested in politics and big business.

We, the voters merely decide who gets the government job. Once we give the politician the job, the money takes over. The politicians are the puppets and as business pulls the strings, the politicians dance around in front of us singing the songs they are paid so well to sing.

Pharmaceutical, oil and gas, mining, steel, aviation, communications, automotive, hi-tech, tobacco and alcohol, banking. **All the business sectors use money, (tons of it) in Washington and Ottawa to influence 'our' politicians to do their bidding.**

Marijuana will never be legal until some significantly big, legal and ultimately taxable, money gets behind it.

Then we'll all be able to get 'Panama Red,' 'Maui Wowie' and 'Pago Pago Purple' at the Seven Eleven and there will be a new type of smoker's cage at the Tim Hortons stores.

They'll be soundproofed, with killer stereo systems inside that play Jimi Hendrix, Pink Floyd and Grateful Dead music all day long. I think their business will go through the roof. People eating a hundred and fifty TimBits for lunch.

I'd keep a close watch for the Seven Eleven lobby and the Tim Hortons/Starbucks lobby on the marijuana thing. If they think there's a buck to be made they'll be among the first to pay the entry fee.

My basic point here is that we should teach our kids to make up their own minds for themselves.

The government and the business sectors don't *really* care what happens to us as individuals. All they want us to do is vote for them, pay our taxes and spend what is left of our money on their products. Period.

As my mother is so fond of telling me, "You're big enough and ugly enough to look after yourself." My grandfather, who actually supported his family during the depression playing poker, once told me, "Trust everybody but cut the cards."

I'd advise you to do the same.

What I think the media should do.

In an effort to produce a balanced perspective to the public, the media should report all the human slaughter that is taking place. Not just AIDS, SARS, the current terrorist activities, the military conditions and the drinking and driving casualties. They should also include a news item every night, where they would report something like:

"Today, 1200 Americans died from smoking and smoking related causes. In fact 25 Americans are going to die before this half hour newscast is even over.

But fortunately for the governments and business interests, 3000 young people started smoking today. Over half of them under the age of 16.

This means that the tobacco industry and the governments had a plus 1800 net gain into their revenue streams. Also, please note that the gain to the tobacco industry is even bigger since the new smokers were all younger than the dead smokers."

It's headlines when people are killed in wars and terrorist attacks, yet we allow this industry to wipe out fifteen hundred Americans and one hundred and twenty three Canadians a day, while all the governments do is blow taxpayers dollars on ads that don't work.

We know how to stop it.

Destroy the profit motive.

Politically and industrially. No lobbying. Make them pay the healthcare tab that their products cause. Don't make the people who don't smoke pay for it. The best way to cure lung cancer and heart disease is to get people to stop smoking but it's just not profitable. No bonuses either to execs until the healthcare bill is paid first.

US-based multinational Philip Morris – the world's biggest cigarette company – was the world's 9th largest advertiser in 1996. They spent more than $3 billion trying to get our kids to start smoking and the worst thing is; it's working.

We *must* destroy the profit motive. They must not be allowed to keep on building their customer base by targeting our children.

In World War II the death toll was 48,000,000. Tobacco has killed way more than that since then and it's still legal!

25% of Canadians over the age of 12 smoke.

40% of them started before the age of 15!

Eighty to one hundred thousand kids start smoking every day and yet, we let the people who do this, do this!

People! I ask y'a.
What is wrong with this picture?

CHAPTER 16

In Retrospect.

Looking back on it all, I've found that some of the best decisions you make in your life are the ones to 'not' do things. My decision to 'not' stay in the Betamax movie rental business was a good one. So was my decision to 'not' do drugs.

But there is not a doubt in my mind that **my decision 'not' to smoke** will ultimately stand as one of **the best decisions** I have ever made in my life. **My decision 'to' smoke is one of the worst.**

It is interesting to notice that the good decisions we make are usually the hardest to execute. The bad ones are easy.

Ultimately, what you need to do is believe.

In yourself.

In your ability to make good decisions. You decide for yourself whether or not you smoke.

Not The Duke.

Not Joe Camel or a coven of lying scumbags at a marketing brainstorming session.

You decide.

It's all about you.

Believe that you must quit and that you can quit.

Do that and Laser therapy will work for you as it did for me. So will most of the methods out there. They just need you to get into it.

Is this the one?

A younger friend of mine is only forty eight years old. His father died of a heart attack when he was fifty three. This friend of mine had a massive heart attack at the age of forty eight.

Two months later he came into my store and we talked about his ordeal. He told me all about it and what he was doing to prevent it from getting any worse. Watching his diet and exercising. He told me his doctors doubted he would survive another one.

"Do you smoke?" I asked him.

He hung his head in shame. "Yes. I do."

"Still smoking?" I asked him.

"I'm down to five or six a day now. After dinner."

"What are you? Crazy? This is obviously killing you. You're going to die if you keep it up."

With a very sad look, he replied, "I know. But I just can't make it through a whole day without one."

I couldn't stop myself. "Every time you light one up you must be asking yourself, 'Is this the one?'"

"Every time."

"Man you know they've got you right where they want you."

"I know. I hope my kids learn from this."

What could I say? He'd almost died at forty eight. He was afraid. He could go anytime he smoked. Yet, he still smokes.

He wants to live.

He's afraid to die.

What is his problem?

His problem is that he doesn't believe he can do it.

Why?

Because **fear alone is not enough.** He isn't **mad** and he hasn't **done all the math.** Add those two factors to the pot and you'll be ready.

How do I know that?

That's how I quit after forty years. **The anger put me over the top. It made me believe** that I could do it. It made me **know** that I had to do it. It gave me my resolve that those people would get no more of my money!

By now you must agree that your smoking experience is similar to mine. We basically smoke for the same reasons. We have the same basic addiction. It's not our bodies. It's our brains. Our brains experience the pleasure.

Our brains believe we're addicted.

You need to change that. Get control. Read Victor Frankl's book, "Man's Search For Meaning."

He survived a Nazi concentration camp by doing just that. Getting control of his brain. And that's how he quit smoking. I read his book and then did some research to find out if he had ever smoked. He did. He had a tough time quitting too. He survived a Nazi death camp and he still had a tough time quitting. Then, he read his own book, took his own advice and used it to help him quit.

He made himself believe he could do it.

Quitting smoking will not be a problem for you. If you decide that it won't be a problem. Al you have to do is:

Get control!

Control of your brain. Do not let the guys at the tobacco company exploit your lack of knowledge and confidence in your self. They think you're a schmuck. They think you are weak minded. And they are using your money to buy yachts and political influence.

If you smoke, you are weak minded.

I know.

I was.

Or at least I believed I was.

Don't do it.

Once you get that control over yourself away from them, you're there.

How do you do that?

Start by gathering facts that build your fear and anger into a belief and a resolve that you have to do it, that you want to do it, that you can do it and then;

Do it!

Like the guy told me and I hope you'll forgive me for belaboring this point. I wouldn't do it if I didn't really, really believe it was so important. By the way, the guy I heard it from, heard it from old Henry Ford.

"If you think you can or you can't, you're probably right."

Henry Ford

Education versus advertising:

Remember this. Most of what you read today is advertising. Not education. Education is the foundation of a good decision. *Not* some ad dreamed up by some dork on Madison Avenue who gets paid to get you to do something that is basically good for him but not necessarily good for you. It's usually a win-lose situation.

The company wins.

You lose.

i.e. You suffer and then you die!

Today I no longer believe in The Duke, the Pepsi generation or any organization that sells food with trans fats in them or the Catholic Church.

I believe in me.

Why?

Because when I walked through that door to the laser treatment I realized that basically, I'm all I've got. Just as you are all you've got. **If you don't believe in yourself, no one else will either.**

I still remember a three-ring binder in the laser people's office. It was full of letters from people who told of their terrible addiction to cigarettes and their experience with the treatment.

When I read the letters I saw myself in every one of them. **They were all written by people who struggled with smoking just as I did.** And they all quit. You should go to this place just to read that book. I'll bet if you do, you'll take the next step.

You will believe. When you believe that you can do it, and throw in the glimmer of hope that comes with that belief, you become armed and dangerous in the eyes of the tobacco industry.

You are now
a smoker who's
ready
to quit!

Reformatting Myself

Authorities say that one year after you quit smoking, you have cut your risk of heart attack in half. After ten years the risk is about the same as that of someone who never smoked. The human body regenerates itself every seven years. (No wonder we get the seven year itch. We've got a whole new body that's never been scratched before.)

When I'm sixty-three I should have a whole new body that is not ravaged by my years of smoking. By then I will have saved almost twenty thousand after-tax dollars at today's prices and will not have smoked 64,000 cigarettes.

I definitely have to be better off because of that. I cannot see what good any of those 64,000 cigarettes would have done except that a grateful government and the tobacco industry would be pleased.

I often wonder how much a cancer victim would have paid for two or three more years of life. Healthy life.

I remember when a dying cancer patient, who was at the end of a three year ordeal with lung cancer, told me that all he really wanted was: *"One day. Just one day where I felt good. All day."*

Seems like so little to ask for, unless you don't have it.

Then it means everything.

I feel pretty good for two reasons. One is that **I know that I beat a bad habit.** The second reason is that **the moment I quit, I started getting healthier.**

Peter Gzowski waited too long. And after all is said and done, maybe I did too. I'll let you know on June 6th 2007.

That's my D-Day.

The big question for you is:

How long are you going to wait?

Another little extra bonus that I did not plan for, surfaced a year after I quit. I have a term life insurance policy to insure that each of my kids will get a nice, new car when I die. It used to cost me two hundred and fifty after-tax dollars a month.

Now it costs me a hundred and sixty.

That's a nice little thousand dollar a year, after tax savings. And my darling children will just have to wait a little longer to get their BMWs.

Up In Smoke.

My big regret is that I didn't quit much earlier. I'd have a brand new BMW 325i convertible now instead of an '85 325i. And an extra sixty grand in my pocket to boot.

Every time I look at a cool hundred thousand dollar car I have to say to myself, **"I could be driving that car now but I smoked it instead."**

But as always, I like to look at the bright side. A forty-year old extremely bad habit that cost me over three thousand after tax dollars per year for forty years, now leaves that money in my jeans for me to spend on things I will be around to enjoy for a while.

What I didn't realize would happen was the change in myself. I now have a renewed sense of purpose and confidence that could only come from doing something that I never believed I could do. It turns out that quitting smoking was just the beginning.

The lighter side?

I have two longtime friends who quit just because I did. They couldn't stand the fact that I had been able to quit while they could not. They said, "Dammit Keelan, if a weak-minded individual like yourself can quit, then I can too."

I loved telling them that they're just afraid of dying before I do.

Afraid that I'd probably wind up fooling around with their wives, living on their yachts and spending all their money.

Those selfish bastards just can't stomach the thought of me having a good time.

Some friends eh?

Not everybody can do it.

My treacherous ex-wife still smokes. Our brilliant, feminazi-dominated, Canadian justice system even forces me to provide her with the money she needs to feed all her addictions. They even took away my driver's license when I hit a bad spot and could not pay. When I told them I couldn't afford to pay, they suggested I quit smoking and give the money I save to her. No kidding. The judge even said it with a seriously straight face.

I'm not wishing that she gets cancer, heart disease or anything else like that. However I have to be honest here and admit that I do fanaticize about her setting herself on fire when she lights up.

Self-immolation.

That would be cool.

Very cool. Burn Baby. Burn.

"Help me make it through the night."

These are some things I've heard quitters say that somehow have stayed with me over the years.

"I'm not going to have one.......today." "You're a puff away from a pack a day." **"I can't have just one because if I do... I'll have ten thousand."**

I've also heard alcoholics say those same things but I've quit drinking almost as many times as I've quit smoking and believe me, **it's harder to quit smoking.** A lot harder.

They are good things to help you through those moments when the urge is upon you, but they are not enough all by themselves. The point here is there is no *one* thing that will do it for you. It's everything coming together that will do it.

Logic, fear and anger coming together to build a level of determination that will put you over the top. Then the support factor can kick in and help you through it. You will find lots of support out there.

The problem I had and most people had was that they went straight to the support part first and I think that without the determination that will come with logic, anger and fear you are doomed to fail or at least you're in for a real ordeal. If the quitting doesn't kill you, your friends or family might.

Now that I've quit, **I know that I won't ever have another cigarette.** I am afraid to. Not just afraid of the death and the pain. **Afraid of losing my self respect.** Afraid of falling back into the clutches of those lying two-faced bastards at the tobacco companies.

I know what will happen to me if I ever start again. I will never stop. In that light, I now describe myself as a recovering nicotine addict. As well as a recovering Catholic, a recovering married guy and a recovering Pepsi drinker.

One day at a time or forever? Either way it's going to be a long, long time.

I've had people tell me that they approach their nicotine addiction recovery the same way an alcoholic would. One day at a time. "I'm not going to have one today."

I can relate to that. Before I quit, the thought of going the rest of my life without a cigarette was a frightful one. The one-day-at-a-time method would be the best way to deal with that kind of fear. The downside for me is the fact that each and every day I would have to deal with the problem. *'Today.'* And then again, *'Tomorrow.'* And every day. *'Forever.'*

That's an awful lot of work for some one who caved in regularly for forty years.

So, where do you go from here?

Okay then. Visualize yourself in the very near future as a non-smoker. Like me, you know you've got it beaten. What would be different about you? What has changed?

You will, like me, realize that stopping smoking is really about two things. Change and control. **You have changed your life and exerted a strong measure of control over it.** Something that you never thought you could do, you have done.

I smoked for forty years and never really ever believed that I would quit. Then I went through the process, fear, anger, logic (the math) and action (I called the laser people).

Once I knew I had beaten it, I realized that I had a new sense of self-confidence, a belief in my ability to do other things. I found myself doing more. I wanted to live longer and be healthier. I believed I could do this and then I went and started doing the things that would help me do it. Now that I was an ex-smoker I believed I had taken a huge step forward towards a longer and healthier life.

I started to eat better, I went to a gym, I rode my bike, I got back into sailboat racing and I cut back on my drinking. (I started having sex four to five times a week. Now I think I'm ready to start dating.)

The drinking part was easy since I enjoyed the way I felt and did not like the way that being half in the bag made me feel. Especially the next morning when I was out on a bike ride or heading for the gym or just basically sitting down to write.

Based on my rates of consumption and activities, in the three years since I have stopped smoking, I have not smoked 7,000 cigarettes, I have not drunk over one hundred and fifty bottles of vodka and rum, I have not consumed almost two thousand cans of Coca Cola. I cannot even begin to estimate the number of french fries I've missed.

I have made 300 trips to the gym, I have ridden my bike over seven thousand miles, I have done over twenty five standup comedy gigs, I have written two books and my 'blockbuster' novel is just around the corner. Last fall I sailed across the Pacific Ocean. I got the chance because despite my age, I am now in good enough shape to do it. I would not have been able to do it five years ago when I was a youngster of 55.

A sixty year old guy with a pack-a-day habit who drinks a lot, never exercises and is thirty pounds overweight would not even think of going on a trip like that, unless he went on a boat named 'Deathwish.'

All of these good things started when I quit smoking. I got a new belief in myself that I could do a lot of things and that I was now going to live long enough to see it through. I saw a reason to try and be healthy enough to do it.

**The best way to describe it is;
self-respect.**

Try it for yourself. Get out of the box you have been living in since you started smoking. You *are not really addicted* to tobacco. Like Jodie explained, you *are addicted* to the endorphin hit. The cigarette is just a way to get the hit. You do not *want* to smoke. What you do *want* to do is find another way to get the endorphin hit.

Riding the bike is great. Sex is by far and away the best endorphin hit they've come up with yet. One great way to get that good feeling is simply that good feeling you'll get when you **know** that you've escaped the clutches of the demon weed.

This belief in yourself, a new sense of self-respect is one of the best feelings there is.

To repeat Mr. Ford,

> "If you think you can or you can't,
> you're probably right."

The big question now is;

What do you think?

CHAPTER 18

Believe It When You See It Or See It When You Believe It?

This is the visualization procedure that I use and many others who have read my story use to get them through any temptation.

Do this and you will be angry and afraid.

Your logical left brain will tell you it's not a smart thing to do.

Then your emotional right brain will tell you that there's no frigging way you're ever going to put one nickel in the hands of those awful people.

I visualize some fat-cat CEO of a tobacco company. He looks like a cross between the evil emperor from Star Wars and Fat Bastard. He is sitting in his corporate ivory tower office looking down on me with gaunt, hollow, sunken, gray, pitiless, small, greedy, lifeless eyes as I grovel at his feet.

Weeping and gnashing my teeth, I throw my money at him pleading and begging for one lousy, rotten, stinking, little puff.

A sinister sneer creeps across his, ugly, pasty, pock-marked face as his nicotine-stained fingers light his cigarette with my five dollar bill.

As he exhales and blows smoke in my face, his victory over me at last complete, his leering smile reveals tar-stained teeth as he says, "You pathetic sucker! I've got y'e right where I want y'e. I'm going to take your money and then I'm going to kill y'e. Slowly and painfully. Then I'm going to do the same thing to your sweet, lovely children."

With that he leans his fat, ugly head back and with quivering jowls, rippling with fat he starts laughing maniacally at me as I moan and wail in agony at his feet.

Let me tell you one thing baby.

That ain't ever going to happen!
End of story.

Speaking of 'end of story', this is the end of this little story:

I've never regretted *not* having a smoke. Never found myself wishing that I'd had that cigarette I was tempted to smoke last night. *"It would have made the night."*

- Let's face it, the only cigarette you really want is the *'the one you want right now.'*
- And you will never regret not having the one you didn't have yesterday. In fact you will feel pretty good for not having given in.
- Remember this, it's never going to be the ones you didn't smoke that you'll regret. It'll always be the ones you did.

If I was still smoking today I'd have smoked another 36,000 cigarettes and spent over $9,000 after tax dollars just for the smokes, plus another three thousand after-tax dollars in life-insurance premiums.

Today I no longer feel like a schmuck.

I think....no wait..... I *know* I did myself a big favour by quitting.

Don't be a schmuck. Don't let your health and your life go up in smoke.

Quit. Now!
Be Free.
FREE AT LAST!

(In case you're interested, Alpha Lifestyle can be reached at 1-800-807-8714. Ask for Jody.)

Is calling Jody the only way?

No. I firmly believe that all of the treatments that are designed to help you quit will work. But if you did spend the extra money to go the laser route, you would be money ahead in a matter of months.

Laser treatment is not the only way to go. It is a good way and for me it was the best way because it worked. The pill, the patch, hypnotism, smoke-ending programs and plain old cold turkey will work if you mix logic, fear and anger along with your pro-active determination to quit.

Once you have acknowledged your anger, fear and the mathematical insanity of it all you can only really decide to do one thing. You have to quit. Now!

Once I did *all* the math, I started to realize that I was 'investing' serious amounts of money in my habit. Money that would easily and obviously be better spent in other areas. The questions you must now surely ask yourself are:

1: Is my decision to smoke a good idea?
2: What are the costs in money and time?
3: Is there a better return on investment for the $100,000 I'm investing in cigarettes?

The conclusion is obvious.

Don't do it!

Now when the subject of quitting comes up it's no longer a question of, "Can I?"

It is now a matter of, "I must!"

When you look back on the ideas, facts and concepts presented in this, you should now be able to make a decision and that is that your decision to keep smoking is not a good one. It's not just bad. It's ridiculous.

Once you realize that, you will immediately start to feel better. The momentum will begin to build. Your addiction is on its way to being beaten. You are on the path to victory.

I can visualize lots of people from my past sitting by their kitchen tables. Drinking coffee, reading the paper, watching TV and smoking. They will in some weird way be comfortable doing this. Resigned to their fate. They believed they were smokers.

Big mistake. Now they're dead. If you give in and start smoking again, you will regret it. **If you are honest with yourself, you regret that you ever started now.**

You need an emotional outburst to get over that. **But, even though it's emotional, it's still the logical thing to do.**

Don't settle for the easy way. It will kill you. There is not one thing out there that will tell you it's the right thing to do.

Life is basically pretty good. You might as well stick around until the end.

To repeat the late Peter Gzowski:

> *"If you've decided to quit, you will: if you haven't, you should get your affairs in order."*

Good luck!
Live long and
live well!